WARBIRDTEC SERIES

VOLUME 34

NORTH AMERICAN
XB-70A VALKYRIE

BY DENNIS R. JENKINS AND TONY LANDIS

specialtypress

PUBLISHERS AND WHOLESALERS

Published by
Specialty Press Publishers and Wholesalers
39966 Grand Avenue
North Branch, MN 55056
United States of America
(800) 895-4585 or (651) 277-1400
http://www.specialtypress.com

Distributed in the UK and Europe by
Midland Publishing
4 Watling Drive
Hinckley LE10 3EY, England
Tel: 01455 233 747 Fax: 01455 233 737
http://www.midlandcountiessuperstore.com

ISBN 1-58007-056-6

Printed in China

Front Cover: *The first XB-70A late in its career sporting the yellow NASA tail stripe. This photo gives an excellent view of the undersurface of the fuselage, showing gear doors, weapons bay, and elevon details.* (Mike Machat Collection)

Back Cover (Left Top): *Air Vehicle 1 returns to the Flight Research Center after a flight on 11 August 1967. Note that all 12 elevons are deployed upward.* (NASA/DFRC Collection)

Back Cover (Right Top): *The XB-70A used over 20,000 square feet of a unique stainless steel honeycomb skin. The skin was formed from three layers – solid (but thin) sheets on the top and bottom, with a porous core between them for light weight and heat resistance.* (North American)

Back Cover (Right Lower): *Air Vehicle 2 under construction in the North American facility in Palmdale, California. The two-position forward windscreen is shown lowered. Also note how the lower radome is attached to the fuselage.* (Gerald H. Balzer Collection)

Title Page: *The two maidens on the ground at Edwards. A/V-2 is in the foreground with the older sister behind her The five degrees of dihedral on the wing seems exaggerated in this photo, but it was nevertheless a noticeable difference between the two aircraft.* (AFFTC History Office Collection)

TABLE OF CONTENTS

NORTH AMERICAN XB-70A VALKYRIE

PREFACE

When one thinks of Mach 3 aircraft, what generally comes to mind is the Lockheed SR-71 or perhaps the MiG 25. But there was another Mach 3 design, one that was a good deal larger and five times heavier than the Blackbird or the Foxbat. Perhaps even more futuristic looking, the North American Aviation XB-70A Valkyrie was the culmination of General Curtis LeMay's quest for the ultimate strategic bomber.

The beginning of the XB-70A story is intertwined with the development of a nuclear-powered bomber – something that could only have been imagined during the 1950s – and a new Mach 3+ interceptor, the F-108 Rapier. All three of these programs were intended to share systems and components, largely as a cost-cutting measure, and the funding nightmare soon unraveled as first the nuclear-powered bomber, then the F-108, were cancelled.

Today, the popular conception of a strategic bomber is the Boeing B-52 Stratofortress. A product of the 1950s, the B-52 recently made the nightly news while carpet-bombing the Taliban in Afghanistan. But what is often overlooked, especially 50 years later, is that the B-52 was the second in a line of "interim" bombers. The first was the Convair B-36, a project begun when it was feared that World War II would need to be conducted entirely from bases within North America. The resulting aircraft was something of a technical triumph, but it was still a piston-powered aircraft born into the beginning of the jet age. Almost as soon as the aircraft appeared, the Strategic Air Command (SAC) began planning to replace it with the newer B-52.

But the B-52 was also born at an awkward time. Although the aircraft that eventually emerged was blessed with swept wings and jet engines – resulting in a bomber that cruised almost twice as fast as the B-36 – it was still a subsonic aircraft at a time when the Air Force desperately wanted to go supersonic. The first supersonic bomber – the Convair B-58 Hustler – was an outgrowth of the preliminary studies that eventually led to the B-70. Sleek looking and fast, it was, at best, a medium bomber. As events turned out, the B-58 – magnificent as it was – became a maintenance nightmare, pushing the state-of-the-art a little too far. Its tenure was very brief.

What Curtis LeMay wanted was an aircraft with the range and payload capabilities of the B-52 and the speed of the B-58. Initially, the replacement for these bombers was to be split between a futuristic nuclear-powered bomber (WS-125A) and a more conventional aircraft

The second XB-70A shows the massive area provided by the delta wing. In addition to providing a great deal of lift on its own, the delta wing used the shock wave produced by the forward tip of the lower fuselage to generate approximately 30 percent more lift – something called "compression lift" by the engineers. This photo provides a good comparison with A/V-1 on the cover. (Rockwell via Jay Miller)

(WS-110A) that used a new high-energy fuel. When these programs began to lag due to technical challenges and funding difficulties, the "interim" B-52 was supplemented with an "improved" B-52 that eventually emerged as the B-52G/H.

There was, however, a dark horse that had been largely dismissed by the user command (SAC), but was high prized by the development commands (ARDC and AMC) and the politicians. The intercontinental ballistic missile (ICBM) was thought to be decades from operations. Then, rather suddenly, breakthroughs that resulted in smaller thermonuclear weapons and reliable guidance systems allowed the Atlas and Titan to be deployed much sooner than had been expected. Manned bombers now appeared – at least to some – to be redundant.

The demise of the WS-125A was a mixed blessing for the B-70 program. It left the Valkyrie as the only manned strategic system under development, helping it gain priority. But the loss of a second funding source for shared systems made the B-70 appear to overrun its budget. The cancellation of the F-108 exasperated this appearance. The deployment of workable ICBMs was the death blow.

Changing political and budgetary climates at first killed the program, then brought it back to life as a two-vehicle test program – sort of a sheep in wolf's clothing. Regardless, when the Valkyrie finally flew,

A/V-2 flies past the parked A/V-1 during an airshow at Edwards AFB, California. The second aircraft is accompanied by a B-58 chase plane (and a T-38 that is just out of the frame). (Tom Rosquin Collection)

it was truly awe-inspiring. Minor technical glitches plagued the program early on, but eventually the aircraft routinely flew at its Mach 3 design speed.

Then tragedy. Air Vehicle 2 was lost in a midair collision during a staged photo shoot after returning from a test flight. XB-70A pilot Al White survived, but copilot Carl Cross, along with F-104 pilot Joe Walker, died in the accident. The program would continue to fly for a while using Air Vehicle 1, but the end was in sight for the largest Mach 3 aircraft ever built. Today the single remaining aircraft is housed at the Air Force Museum in Dayton, Ohio – just as awe-inspiring as the day she was rolled out in Palmdale , California, 40 years ago.

The authors would like to thank: Tony Accurso, Gerald H. Balzer, Randy Cannon, Joe Cotton, Archie DiFante at the AFHRA, Fitzhugh "Fitz" Fulton, Michael H. Gorn and Dill Hunley at DFRC, Marty Isham, Denny Lombard, Michael J. Lombardi at the Boeing Archives, Betty Love at DFRC, Scott Lowther at Aerospace Projects Review, Yancy Mailes, Don Mallick, Jay Miller, Doug Nelson at the AFFTC Museum, Ken Neubeck, Terry Panopalis, Charles E. Rogers at AFFTC, Tom Rosquin, Mick Roth, Jim Tuttle, Jack Weber at AFMC, and Jim Young in the AFFTC History Office.

Dennis R. Jenkins
Cape Canaveral, Florida

Tony Landis
Lancaster, California

A/V-1 during taxi tests at Palmdale prior to first flight. At 500,000 pounds, the Valkyrie was the heaviest aircraft built at the time. This posed some challenges for systems that had little to do with the bomber's Mach 3 speed potential – such as brakes, which tended to chatter during low-speed stops. Taxiing the XB-70A took some getting used to since the pilots sat high and far in front of the landing gear. (Tony Landis Collection)

ANTECEDENTS

The building of the XB-70A probably ranks as one of the most convoluted processes in modern defense procurement. Initial studies were hampered by limitations in the state-of-the-art, but ultimately resulted in the development of the Convair B-58 Hustler, the world's first supersonic bomber.

Later studies were intertwined with at least three other programs. An effort to develop a nuclear-powered bomber (NPB) under WS-125A – itself an outgrowth of the very expensive Nuclear Energy for the Propulsion of Aircraft (NEPA) and Aircraft Nuclear Propulsion (ANP) programs – provided an unnecessary diversion of funds and interest from the less-technically advanced WS-110A chemically-powered bomber (CPB) program that eventually became the B-70. A fleeting desire to build a reconnaissance version of the new bomber as WS-110L fell by the wayside as other programs promised more significant advances, but again diverted resources from the B-70 for a short time. The F-108 interceptor was seen as a second funding source for many WS-110 and WS-125 sub-systems (including the J93 engines), and its premature cancellation forced a major funding crisis upon the B-70 program.

Perhaps most significantly, one of the competitors for funds was the intercontinental missile program. At first it was not obvious whether the resulting weapon would be a large cruise missile or a ballistic missile. In fact, it was not readily apparent that the concept would work at all. Ultimately, break-throughs in building smaller thermonuclear weapons and accurate guidance systems allowed the development of the Atlas and Titan intercontinental ballistic missiles (ICBM) as well as the Thor intermediate range ballistic missile (IRBM) and the Navy's Polaris (and later, Poseidon and Trident) submarine launch ballistic missiles (SLBM). These largely spelled the end for both the long-range cruise missiles and the manned bomber programs.

Initially the ballistic missiles were given little chance of immediate success since the size of the thermonuclear warheads was so large. However, much sooner than expected, the warheads became smaller and missiles like the Atlas became possible. This is the ninth Atlas-B test vehicle on its pad at Cape Canaveral AFS, Florida, on 17 November 1958. (45th Space Wing History Office)

Once Upon a Time ...

As early as 1947 the Air Force had begun developing requirements for a supersonic intercontinental bomber. In early 1948 two companies, Boeing and Consolidated-Vultee Aircraft (usually called Convair), received Air Force contracts to study the possibilities of a supersonic bomber. Over the next four years these and subsequent studies evolved into a competition that resulted in the Convair B-58 Hustler medium bomber.[1]

On 30 March 1953 the Strategic Air Command (SAC) defined its future aircraft requirements in a letter to Air Force Headquarters. SAC believed that manned flight to high altitudes and long ranges should be "... at all times a priority objective of the Air Force development program." The on-going intercontinental missile program was not expected to yield an operational weapon in the foreseeable future, due in large part to the anticipated size and weight of the thermonuclear warhead. Therefore, SAC called for the design and production of a high-performance long-range bomber to follow the B-52. The projected bomber was to employ "... the longest range, highest altitude, and greatest speed (in that order of priority), capable of attainment in the time period under consideration and consistent with requirements for military payload and defensive systems."[2]

The bureaucracy was apparently much more responsive in 1953, and on 1 May 1953 contract AF33(616)-2070 was issued to Boeing for a one-year study of an advanced strategic weapons system. The requirement was for a manned aircraft possessing intercontinental range while carrying a 50,000-pound thermonuclear payload. It was to become operational in the 1960–1965 timeframe.

Boeing presented their preliminary results on 22 January 1954, leveraging heavily off developments made in the NEPA/ANP programs. The problem was that the early nuclear engines – although being very long-ranged – were not expected to be powerful enough to push a large aircraft through the sound barrier. In order to gain more speed for short periods of time, Boeing augmented the nuclear engines with a pair of conventional turbojets (called chemical engines although they burned standard JP-4). The nuclear engines would provide a long-range subsonic cruise capability, while the chemical engines would produce additional thrust for a short supersonic dash over the target. In March 1954, Boeing presented their final report on a chemically-augmented nuclear-powered aircraft; Convair and Lockheed, under contracts with the Office of Aircraft Nuclear Propulsion, submitted similar data.[3]

Then the unexpected occurred. By May 1954 the National laboratories had managed to reduce the size and weight of the so-called "H-bombs" to the point that they no longer represented a daunting payload. At about the same time, breakthroughs at MIT and other research institutes allowed the development of accurate and compact guidance systems. These technical advances provided a strong impetus to accelerate development of a new manned strategic bomber. Perhaps unfortunately, they also provided the break that was necessary for the development of workable ballistic missiles, which eventually replaced the manned bomber as the deterrent system of choice.

The initial studies for a supersonic bomber resulted in the development of the Convair B-58 Hustler. The aircraft was much faster than any other bomber in the world at the time, but it had relatively short legs and was a maintenance nightmare. After less than a decade in service, SAC retired them. (U.S. Air Force)

WARBIRD**TECH**
S E R I E S

Since these developments largely invalidated most of the concepts investigated by Boeing for the previous year, a 12-month extension was awarded as Project MX-2145. The specifications included 20,000- and 40,000-pound payloads, a radius of action between 3,000 and 5,000 miles, refueling (if necessary) outside the Soviet early-warning system, and a cruise altitude above 50,000 feet while over enemy territory.[4]

At the time, the Air Force had an independent engine program that developed new power plants largely separately from the programs that would eventually use them. In the fall of 1954 the Power Plant Laboratory at Wright Field began investigating possible engines for the new bomber. Two turbojets were especially promising – the Allison J89 combined an efficient subsonic cruise potential with a supersonic dash capability; and the all-supersonic Pratt & Whitney J91 (JT9) being developed to support the ANP program. Two other engines were less seriously considered – the General Electric X84 (TF31) turbofan and the ambitious dual-cycle Wright J67 being developed for the Republic XF-103 interceptor, a unit in which the afterburner transformed into a ramjet at about Mach 2.25.

In early October 1954, the Air Force published General Operational Requirement No. 38 (GOR 38). The document was brief – it called for an intercontinental manned bomber to replace the B-52 by 1963. On 28 October 1954, the Air Research and Development Command (ARDC) presented General Curtis E. LeMay, the Commander-in-Chief of SAC, with four advanced concepts. The

Little was ever declassified about the WS-125A project, although this drawing of one of the Convair designs has circulated for years. The two nuclear engines were located in the fuselage; the underwing engines were conventional "chemical" turbojets used to provide extra power for the supersonic dash. (General Dynamics)

first was a conventional chemically-powered bomber available in 1963 with a combat radius of 3,000 nm. This bomber was to cruise at Mach 0.9, but would penetrate the last 750-1,000 nm at speeds between Mach 1.5 and Mach 2.5 and an altitude of 50,000 to 60,000 feet. The second alternative was the nuclear-cruise and chemical-dash concept initially devised by Boeing. Also available in 1963, this design carried a much higher development risk than the first concept. The third idea was the same as the second, except the operational date was slipped to 1965, somewhat easing the development risk. The last alternative was a nuclear-cruise aircraft with a nuclear-dash capability, but it would not be available until 1968–1970, at the earliest.

In choosing the second alternative, LeMay reaffirmed the urgency of the 1963 date – this was a year after the last B-52 was expected to be manufactured, and would represent the end-of-life for the earlier model B-52s. Preliminary studies by Boeing, Convair, and Lockheed had all shown that a chemically-augmented nuclear-powered bomber could be designed and built, although the supersonic dash capability would likely be less than 750 nm.

However, LeMay was nothing if not a realist. To guard against unexpected problems in the nuclear program, he wanted a chemically-powered

bomber developed in parallel as a separate program. Although sound from a military perspective, LeMay's proposal was expensive – the cost of developing both systems was estimated at $3,900 million. On 9 December 1954 the Wright Air Development Center (WADC) recommended against this proposal and suggested that all efforts should be concentrated on the nuclear-program. Ignoring this advice, on 29 December 1954 the Air Council decided to pursue two simultaneous but independent development programs for a chemically-powered bomber (WS-110A) and a nuclear-powered bomber (WS-125A). Both were to be operational by 1963.

In light of the Air Council decision, and in response to GOR 38, on 18 February 1955 the ARDC issued Study Requirement No. 22 (SR 22) for a chemically-powered bomber capable of cruising at Mach 0.9 and possessing "maximum possible speed" during a 1,000 nm penetration while carrying a 50,000-pound load. The desired radius of action was 4,000 nm, generally reflecting the preference SAC had always shown* for range over high speed.[5]

Around the same time, the Air Force released GOR 96 for an intercontinental reconnaissance system very similar to WS-110A. This followed LeMay's practice of procuring a reconnaissance version of each post-war strategic bomber (there had been RB-36s, RB-45s, RB-47s, and even some early RB-52s). The reconnaissance system was identified as Weapon System 110L. Logically enough, the two systems were soon combined, becoming WS-110A/L.[6]

The number of engines under consideration grew in 1955 and 1956. Wright had come up with an improved J67 called the TJ32C4. Pratt & Whitney offered an improved J75. General Electric proposed at least two advanced versions of the J79 – the company-designated X207, which raised the engine's thrust from about

15,000 to 18,000-lbf, and the 20,700-lbf X275. Still the Allison J89 and the Pratt & Whitney J91 were the only two candidates actively under development by the Air Force.

CHOOSING A CONTRACTOR

On 22 March 1955 the Air Force issued GOR 82, superseding the earlier GOR 38; on 15 April SR 22 was revised to match. The requirements lowered the radius of action to 3,000 nm and the dash distance to 750 nm in an effort to preserve the 1963 operational date. However, it is

noteworthy that GOR 82 called for the maximum possible "supersonic" speed in the combat zone as opposed to the earlier "maximum possible speed" – a subtle but significant difference.[7]

In April 1955 the WADC proposed slipping the operational date to mid-1964 in order to reduce fiscal and development risks. At the time, the estimated cost to develop and field an operational wing of the new aircraft was $2,500 million. This assumed that the nuclear-powered bomber would also be developed, that the new engine for the chemically-powered bomber would be paid for by the normal Air Force engine program, and that certain subsystem development costs would be shared by the WS-125A program.[8]

On 16 July 1955, six airframe contractors – Boeing, Convair, Douglas, Lockheed, Martin, and North American – were selected to bid on the preliminary WS-110A/L studies. Convair and Lockheed were soon awarded WS-125A contracts and elected not to compete for the seemingly less-challenging WS-110A/L contract. Douglas and Martin, along with another division of Convair, were busy developing missiles and did not want to dilute that effort.* Therefore, the WS-110A competition narrowed to two companies, Boeing and North American Aviation.

Separately, on 6 October 1955 the Air Force released GOR 114 for the WS-202A Long-Range Interceptor, Experimental (LRIX) program. Surprisingly, no record of a competition exists, but on 6 June 1957 North American received a letter contract for an all-weather two-man, twin-engine interceptor to be operational

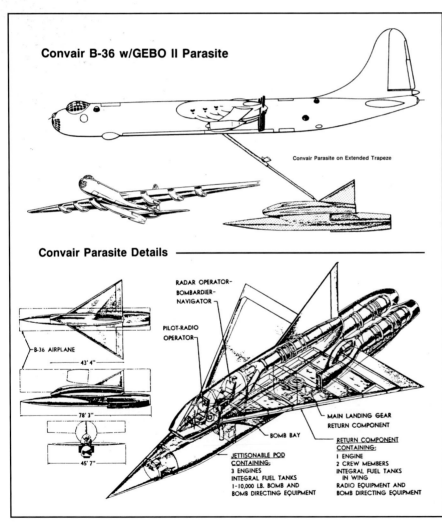

The Convair GEBO studies were among the more bizarre attempts to create a supersonic intercontinental bomber. A small two-part parasite would be "towed" by a B-36 to a location off the Soviet coast, then released for a high-speed bomb run against its target. (Jay Miller Collection)

* Convair was developing the Atlas ICBM; Douglas the Thor IRBM; and Martin the Titan ICBM.

Republic XF-103

In early 1948 Alexander Kartveli at Republic Aviation began designing the Mach 3 AP-44A all-weather high altitude defense fighter – less than a year after the first XS-1 supersonic flight,. Republic sent preliminary data to the Air Force in January 1951, and in September received a Phase I development contract for WS-204A. Although the entire aircraft was extremely futuristic, perhaps its most notable feature was the Wright J67 dual-cycle turbojet engine. The engine installation provided a large bypass duct that fed air directly into the afterburner, allowing it to function as a ramjet at high speed.[11]

A full-scale mockup was reviewed on 2 March 1953, and resulted primarily in replacing the pilot's canopy with a flush cockpit equipped with a periscope. An 18-month extension of the Phase I contract was used for further studies of titanium fabrication, high-temperature hydraulics, escape capsules, and periscopic sights.

Although development money was hard to come by, the Air Force decided that the Mach 3 interceptor held so much promise that they continued to fund the program despite a variety of technical problems. By July 1954 the program had advanced to the point that the Air Force awarded Republic a contract to manufacture three prototypes. However, various technical problems continued, and the low funding level made it difficult to apply sufficient resources to overcome them, so solutions were elusive.[12]

In early 1957 the program was cut back to a single prototype and two flight engines, but little progress had been made by 21 August 1957 when the XF-103 prototype and Wright engine were cancelled entirely. The program had cost $104 million over nine years.[13]

The XF-103 was probably the first serious Mach 3 design proposed in the United States. This mockup has a conventional cockpit canopy; the final design used a flush canopy equipped with a periscope. The first flight vehicle was under construction when the program was cancelled. (Republic via Ken Neubeck)

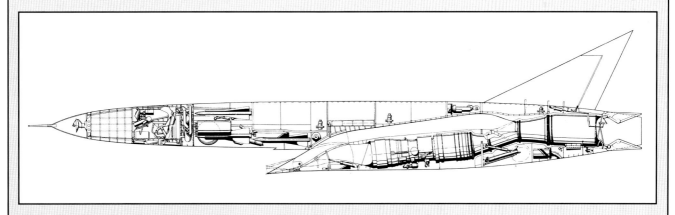

Alexander Kartveli selected an innovative engine concept where the afterburner was physically separated from the Wright J67 turbojet. At speeds above Mach 2.5, inlet air was routed around the J67 directly to the afterburner, fuel was added, and the unit became a ramjet. This eliminated the temperature restrictions inherent in turbojet engines. The fire control system and GAR-1 (AIM-4) Falcon missile armament would have been identical to that installed on the Convair F-102 Delta Dagger. The basic J67 was briefly considered for use on the early WS-110A concepts. (Republic via Charles E. Rogers)

NORTH AMERICAN XF-108

The Republic XF-103 effort was in obvious difficulties by 1955, but the Air Force still felt a need for an interceptor with higher performance than was expected from the upcoming Convair F-102B (F-106). On 6 October 1955 the Air Force released GOR 114 for the Long-Range Interceptor, Experimental (LRIX), which was largely a less technically demanding follow-on to the struggling XF-103. North American won the compeition over Lockheed and Northrop, and on 6 June 1957 received a letter contract for an all-weather two-man, twin-engine interceptor.[14]

The aircraft would be capable of at least Mach 3 at 70,000 feet. After cruising more than 1,150 miles at its best (probably subsonic) speed, the F-108 was to have sufficient fuel for 5 minutes of combat at Mach 3, then be able to cruise home. Alternately, the aircraft could scramble 390 miles at Mach 3 and engage in 10 minutes of Mach 3 combat. To achieve this required a large aircraft – the F-108 was 85 feet long, spanned 53 feet, and was 22 feet high. The gross weight was 102,000 pounds, with a combat weight projected at 73,000 pounds. The wing area was 1,400 square feet.[15]

The F-108 mockup was inspected on 26 January 1959, and the aircraft was named Rapier on 15 May 1959. First flight was expected in March 1961 with operational aircraft being delivered beginning in 1963. Although the Air Force had a stated requirement for 480 of the aircraft, fiscal problems resulted in the program being cancelled on 23 September 1959.[16]

The Hughes Aircraft Corporation was developing the advanced AN/ASG-18 fire-control system for the new interceptor. The F-108 would carry three GAR-9 (AIM-47) Super Falcon missiles in a rotary launcher just aft of the cockpit. These missiles could be fitted with large conventional or small nuclear warheads. Even after the XF-108 was cancelled, development of the fire control system and missile continued, eventually finding brief use on the three Lockheed YF-12A interceptor prototypes. The performance of the system was, by all accounts, very successful. The basic system architecture and many of the lessons learned from the development effort were later applied to the AN/AWG-9 and AIM-54 developed for the Grumman F-14 Tomcat.

Other subcontractors involved in the XF-108 program included Convair (wing), Marquardt (air induction control system), Hamilton Standard (air conditioning and pressurization), the Federal Division of the International Telephone & Telegraph Company (mission and traffic control system), and the Electronic Specialty Company (antennas).

An artist concept of the F-108. A later version would trade the true delta wing for something resembling a "cranked" wing. (Terry Panopalis Collection)

The XF-108 mockup as it appeared during the formal Air Force review. The aircraft promised performance roughly equivalent to that later achieved by the Lockheed YF-12A. (Terry Panopalis Collection)

in 1963. The aircraft was to be powered by the same engine selected for the WS-110A, and would also share many of the subsystems, such as escape capsules, navigation systems, hydraulics, etc. This is particularly interesting when you note that the letter contract was issued almost six months before North American won the WS-110A competition.[9]

On 8 November 1955 the Air Force awarded letter contracts to both Boeing and North American for the Phase I development of Weapon System 110A/L. Each contractor had to provide models, drawings, specifications, reports, conduct wind tunnel tests, and construct a mockup within two years. Boeing signed contract AF33(600)-31802 on 15 March 1956; North American followed on 16 April with contract AF33(600)-31801.[10]

Design Proposals

Not surprisingly the preliminary designs submitted by Boeing and North American in mid-1956 were quite different. The Boeing concept was a fairly conventional swept-wing aircraft powered by four 27,070-lbf (in afterburner) General Electric X275 turbojets. The North American design used six 26,425-lbf versions of the X275 and somewhat resembled a scaled-up Navaho missile.* Still, in order to meet the range requirements several features of the two designs were remarkably similar. Both aircraft would weigh some 750,000 pounds and use "floating wing panels" (a term coined by Boeing but ultimately applied to both

---

* The North American SM-64A Navaho (WS-104A) was a vertically launched, air-breathing, intercontinental surface-to-surface, delta-wing missile, with a length of 87 feet and a diameter of 6.5 feet. Production was canceled in July 1957 because of budgetary and technical problems and the success of the ICBM program. The Navaho development cost over $600 million, but much of the work performed found later application on other programs, including the Space Shuttle.

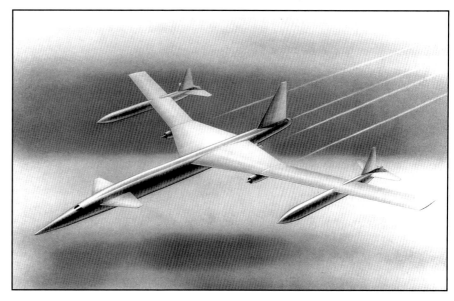

Floating wingtips. The Boeing Model 724-13 used two Model 724-1001 wingtips to carry extra fuel during the subsonic cruise portion of the WS-110A mission. (Boeing via the Terry Panopalis Collection)

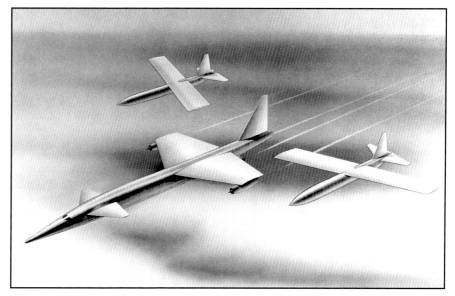

design) to house additional fuel. Each of the 190,000-pound (loaded) panels was the size of a B-47 medium bomber and would carry fuel for the trip to the target. When the fuel was exhausted the panels would be jettisoned – without the panels the main aircraft would be capable of dash speeds in excess of Mach 2.[17]

The floating panel concept had first been put forward by Dr. Richard Vogt, a German scientist who came to the United States after World War II. Vogt proposed to increase the range of an aircraft by attaching two "free floating" panels to carry extra fuel. This could be accomplished without undue structural weight

penalties if the extensions were free to articulate and were self-supported by their own aerodynamic lift. In addition, the panels would effectively increase the aspect ratio of the overall wing, providing a significant reduction in wing drag. Therefore, as the theory went, the extra fuel was being carried "for free" by the more efficient wing and the extra fuel increased the range of the aircraft. Other potential uses for this concept quickly became apparent. The one that sparked the most interest was for a bomber to carry two escort fighters, one on each wingtip. The Germans had apparently experimented with the idea during late 1944 and the U.S. Air Force began similar experiments in 1949 using a Douglas C-47A and Culver PQ-14B. To further evaluate the concept, two projects, TIP TOW and Tom-Tom, attached jet fighters to the wingtips of a B-29 and a B-36. However, it was finally decided that the experiments were too dangerous after a three-aircraft EF-84D/EB-29A/EF-84D array crashed as a unit on 24 April 1953, killing everybody on all three aircraft.[18]

This was the North American concept that used floating wingtips. Note the location of the canard. The Air Force was concerned that the canard restricted forward visibility to the point of being dangerous during takeoff and landing. (above: Gerald H. Balzer Collection; below: Terry Panopalis Collection)

Nevertheless, the floating wing tip concept was strongly supported by the ARDC during 1956 as a likely method of achieving the desired range for WS-110A. In September 1956 an ARDC study group reported that floating wing tips appeared to be a "very promising means of extending the subsonic range of aircraft from 30% to 100%."[19]

The Boeing and North American preliminary designs had another factor in common – both were considered unsatisfactory. Upon seeing the concepts, Curtis LeMay is reported as saying "These aren't airplanes, they are three-ship formations." At roughly 750,000 pounds fully loaded, there

were no runways in the world that could support the proposed aircraft. The floating wing tips seemed impractical since they extended the wingspan to nearly 300 feet and could not be accommodated on any airfield. Additionally, many in the Air Force had grown wary of the floating panel concept after the 1953 TIP TOW crash. In September 1956, a disappointed Air Staff recommended that both contractors "return to the drawing board."[20]

SELECTING A CONTRACTOR

During late 1956 and the first part of 1957 the possibility of an all-supersonic mission concept appeared to become more feasible. The development of turbojet engines with reduced fuel consumption in supersonic flight was one advance, and basic research in aerodynamics at the NACA Ames Aeronautical Laboratory allowed the contractors to refine their airframe configurations to varying degrees. At the same time, the Navaho missile began demonstrating the feasibility of extended Mach 3 flight.

By March 1957 it seemed almost certain that the new weapon system could be an all-supersonic cruise vehicle as opposed to a "split-mission" aircraft. The designers had discovered that if the entire aircraft (engines, air induction system, and airframe) was designed for Mach 3 flight then the range would compare favorably with that of a subsonic vehicle. The engine contractors seemed to support this theory. Both airframe contractors also concluded that, as suggested by the Air Force, a boron-based high-energy fuel used in the engine afterburner would provide a 10–15 percent increase in range over conventional JP-4. This extra range, however, would come

An evolved Boeing Model 724-16 shows that engines have been added to each of the Model 724-1000 floating wingtips, and that an additional engine has been added under each wing of the main aircraft. (Boeing via the Terry Panopalis Collection)

at a significant cost in terms of fuel system complication and engine design. (See Appendix C for a brief history of the HEF program).[21]

In the spring of 1956 there had been three engines under active consideration – the Allison J89, Pratt & Whitney J91, and General Electric X275. The race became a two-way contest after the all-supersonic mission model was adopted, effectively ruling out the J89 that was optimized for subsonic cruise. The two remaining engines were gradually tailored to the anticipated needs of the advanced bomber. The giant J91 was scaled down and transformed into a Mach 3 engine; as a Navy-sponsored project it became the J58 that would go on to power the Lockheed Blackbirds. The General Electric X275 (a scaled-up J79) became the X279 when it was optimized for Mach 3 cruising and eventually became the J93.[22]

Since both of the airframe contractors favored the General Electric engine over that from Pratt & Whitney, on 26 July 1957 the Air Force issued letter contract AF33(600)-

35824 for the development of the X279E. The engine was officially designated XJ93-GE-1 on 25 September 1957. The definitive contract was signed on 14 May 1958. The new engine was a medium-pressure-ratio turbojet with a mass airflow of approximately 220 pounds per second and a potential speed of more than Mach 3. Interestingly, no mention was made of high-energy fuels.[23]

Having sufficiently studied the concept, on 30 August 1957 the Air Force told the airframe contractors that a winner would be selected after a 45-day competitive design period. On 18 September, the Air Force issued a final revised specification that called for a cruise speed of Mach 3.0 to Mach 3.2, an altitude of 70,000 to 75,000 feet, a range of 6,100 to 10,500 miles, and a gross weight between 475,000 and 490,000 pounds. The final Boeing and North American proposals would be due in 30 days.[24]

The resulting designs were for much more realistic aircraft. They were about the same length as the B-52,

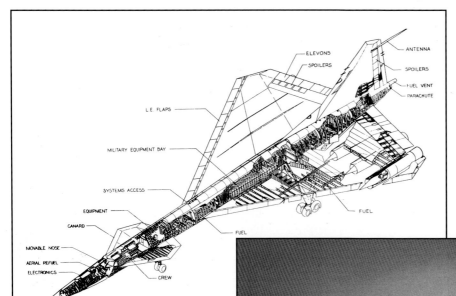

The slightly later Boeing Model 804-4 added a larger canard that was used – much like North American's entry – only for trim at high speeds. Note the spoiler panels integrated into the sides of the vertical stabilizer, and the large antenna protruding from the trailing edge of the vertical. The wing was equipped with leading edge flaps. Note that the basic engine placement would later be used years the Model 733 SST. (The Boeing Company)

but had slightly less wingspan, were a little taller, and weighed about 10 percent more. Both aircraft were designed to use existing B-52 bases and to be maintained by existing skills available to SAC.

The Boeing design was a delta wing aircraft with retractable canards that

The original Boeing Model 804-1 used small retractable canards for trimming, but these were found to be unsatisfactory as wind tunnel testing progressed. (Terry Panopalis Collection)

generally resembled an overgrown Bomarc missile. Six General Electric

J93 engines in individual pods under the wing burned boron fuel in the afterburners only (JP-4 was used in the main combustor). Boeing proposed a titanium hot-structure much like what would appear on the Lockheed Blackbirds. The gross weight was 499,500 pounds, a little over the requirement but deemed acceptable.

The North American aircraft featured a large delta wing, a forward canard, and an airframe constructed from a newly-developed stainless steel honeycomb material. The outer 20 percent of each wingtip could be folded downward to provide additional stability at high speeds, allowing smaller (with less drag) vertical stabilizers. Like Boeing, North American opted for six J93 boron engines, but housed them side-by-side in a single large box-like structure under the wing. Gross weight was estimated at 483,000 pounds.

The Air Force evaluation group,[*] numbering about 60 members, reviewed the North American proposal during the last week of October; Boeing had their turn during the first week of November. The North American proposal was unanimously found to be superior to Boeing's, and the results were presented to the Air Council on 15 December. The Air Force formally announced North American's selection on 23 December 1957.[25]

Part of why North American had won was that the Air Force believed a bit of aerodynamic voodoo included in the proposal. Without the floating wingtips to provide additional range, North American engineers had poured through every aerodynamic study they could find, looking for anything that could be applied to the new bomber. What they "discovered" during the literature search was a report written by NACA[†] researchers Alfred J. Eggers and Clarence A. Syverston on 5 March 1956. Entitled *Aircraft Configurations Developing High Lift/Drag Ratios at High Supersonic Speeds*, the paper suggested that a high-speed aircraft could be designed such that the lift-over-drag ratio could be increased in supersonic flight by relying on pressure from the shock wave impinging on the lower surfaces of the wings. North American exploited this "compression lift" theory by using a wedge-shaped box inlet under the leading edge of the wing to create a positive pressure behind the main shock wave that reacted on the large

A very early artist concept of the North American proposal shows a single vertical stabilizer, but is generally representative of the final design. Note that a large portion of the wingtip is shown folded here, unlike the 20-percent semispan that was actually proposed. (The Boeing Company)

underwing surface. Since there was no equivalent pressure wave on top of the wing to cancel it out, roughly a 30-percent increase in lift was available with no drag penalty. This would substantially increase the range – if it worked.[26]

GETTING STARTED

On 24 January 1958 North American signed contract AF33(600)-36599 for the Phase I development of the WS-110A/L. At the time, the Air Force was expecting that the first operational wing of 30 aircraft could be available in late 1965. The aircraft component of WS-110A was designated B-70 in February 1958.

Less than a month after contract award, in February 1958, the Air Force cancelled the development of WS-110L since it believed that "other systems" could better satisfy the reconnaissance requirements in the 1965 time frame. Contrary to popular opinion, the "other system" was probably Lockheed's hydrogen-

powered Project SUNTAN since the Blackbird (A-12) was still a year or two in the future. Or perhaps the Air Force was referring to the CORONA satellite program that would begin flying in 1960. In either case, there would be no reconnaissance version of the B-70.[27]

At the same time that the reconnaissance requirement was being deleted, an 18-month acceleration of the B-70 program was being planned. This change scheduled first flight for December 1961 and the first operational wing for August 1964. Although this would bring the aircraft closer to the 1963 date desired by LeMay, the change would cost an additional $165 million. The Air Staff approved the accelerated plan in principle on 19 March 1958.[28]

With a contract in hand, North American began issuing subcontracts for major portions of the B-70. Westinghouse was to design the defensive electronics system that would include advanced infrared and radar

---

[*] For the first time in an Air Force procurement, the using command (SAC, in this case) was allowed to participate in the evaluation. Previously this had been limited to the Air Research and Development Command and the Air Materiel Command. Due to the success of the 3-team evaluation group, the Air Force changed its source selection procedures, the using command becoming an integral part of the selecting process.

[†] The National Advisory Committee for Aeronautics (always pronounced en-aay-cee-aay, never "naka") became the nucleus of the National Aeronautics and Space Administration on 1 October 1958.

This is the North American design that was considered the competition winner. Note the large vertical stabilizers and the relatively small portion of the wingtip that folded. The canard is also much larger and differently shaped than the one actually built. Still, the aircraft is clearly a Valkyrie. (The Boeing Company)

warning receivers, as well as sophisticated jamming equipment. General Electric would be responsible for the jam-proof forward and side-looking radars that would eventually be hooked up to the IBM AN/ASQ-28 offensive bombing-navigation subsystem (which was originally under separate Air Force contract, but later came under North American's purview). The airframe was divided between Boeing (wings), Chance-Vought (tail and elevons), Lockheed (aft fuselage) and various North American divisions. Sperry was providing a twin-gyro star tracker while Sundstrand designed the secondary power system. Cleveland Pneumatic provided the landing gear and Oster the engine instrumentation. And on it went – North American was well aware that spreading the wealth ensured that every Congressman and Senator would want to continue funding the program.

Although the General Electric engine had been conceived for the B-70, the Air Force intended to use the initial J93-GE-1 on the F-108 interceptor because that program was further along in its development. On 13 January 1958 General Electric suggested a growth version of the –1 engine that featured higher internal and exhaust temperatures and used air-cooled turbine blades. This engine would produce slightly more thrust at Mach 3 and also provide better specific fuel consumption, something more important to the B-70 than to the F-108. On 18 April 1958, the growth version of the engine was officially designated XJ93-GE-3 and programmed for the B-70. However, planning was finally underway for a –5 engine using high-energy fuels.

By July 1958 General Electric reported that it would greatly sim-

plify development if the –3 engine was used in the F-108 and early B-70 aircraft, pending availability of the boron-burning –5 engine. Notable logistics support savings could also be achieved by using one engine, since a number of major components in the –1 and –3 were not interchangeable. As far as the F-108 was concerned, North American believed that the improved thrust and specific fuel consumption performance of the –3 engine compensated adequately for its 240 pounds of extra weight. The Air Force made the idea official on 8 September 1958; only the four –1 engines already being manufactured would be built, mainly to provide an early testing opportunity. All further effort would concentrate on the –3 engine. Interestingly, there was still no official –5 development effort authorized, although General Electric and North American continued to plan around the high energy engine.[29]

Like most combat aircraft of the period, the name for the B-70 was decided by a contest, not by a corporate advertising agency. In this case, SAC held an Air Force-wide contest that attracted 20,000 entries. The winner was Valkyrie, from the Maidens[*] in Norse mythology. The name became official on 3 July 1958.

In the summer of 1958 the Air Force again considered the possibility of supporting the Pratt & Whitney J58

---

* Valkyries (from the Old Norse Valkyrjr, "choosers of the slain") in Norse mythology were the daughters of the principal god Odin – often called Odin's maidens. At his bidding, they flew on their horses over the fields of battle to choose the souls of the heroic dead, which they carried off to Valhalla, Odin's banquet hall in the heavenly realm of Asgard. There the warriors became members of the Einherjar, Odin's companions and fighting band. The Valkyries were depicted as young, beautiful, but fierce women who dressed splendidly in full armor and swords when riding their horses. Valkyries also had the power to determine who would be the victors and who the defeated in such conflicts. Belief in the existence of magic horsewomen from heaven was widespread in Scandinavia and Germanic cultures, though they were called by different names.

as a backup engine for the J93, but elected not to. It was decided, however, to contribute a small amount of funding to the Navy's J58 program during FY59 just to keep the door open. By late 1958 General Electric was making progress on the J93 engine. Two versions were now officially being developed – the J93-GE-3 burned JP-4 and was intended for the F-108 and prototype B-70s, and the J93-GE-5 that burned HEF-3 boron fuel in the afterburner and was intended for production B-70s.

The J93 engine was based on a "module" concept where most all accessories (hydraulic pumps, generators, etc.) were moved off the engine and onto the airframe. This was an attempt to protect the engine from damage should an accessory fail (which was a fairly common occurrence at the time), and also to simply the production and installation of the engines. Each engine had a mechanical take-off shaft that transmitted power to an airframe-mounted accessory drive gearbox, to which the accessories were attached as needed. This also allowed a single engine configuration to be used in either the F-108 or B-70 since it was no longer necessary to worry about the placement of accessories to fit into the engine bay. Taking the idea one step further, General Electric proposed delivering engines to operational units that were completely assembled, tuned, and ready to be installed – no run-ups or other testing would be required after delivery to operational units.

In the fall of 1958, the B-70 program received a severe jolt when Air Force Chief of Staff General Thomas D. White announced that the planned acceleration was no longer viable because of funding limitations. The first flight would be delayed to January 1962, with the first operational wing not appearing before August 1965 at the earliest. White also told his staff that the Eisenhower Administration believed that no large sums of money should be committed to the B-70 program before the prototype had proven itself. It was the beginning of a slow death.[30]

This later artist concept seems to have ignored the folding wingtips altogether. Note the shape of the vertical stabilizer leading edges. (Gerald H. Balzer Collection)

[1] Air Force Development Directive 00034, 26 February 1952, in the files of the AFMC History Office; Letter, Colonel V.R. Haugen, Chief of the Weapons Systems Division, WADC, to the Commander ARDC, subject: Strategic Bomber/Recon Weapons Systems Development Program, 8 October 1952. In the files of the AFMC History office. [2] Letter, Major General T. S. Power, Vice Commander SAC to the Director of Requirements, USAF, subject: Requirement for Long Range Strategic Bombardment Aircraft, 30 March 1953. In the files of the AFMC History office. [3] Marcelle Size Knaack, *Post-World War II Bombers*, (Washington DC: Office of Air Force History, 1988), pp. 559-560. [4] Ibid, p. 559. [5] Ibid, pp. 560-561. [6] Ibid, p. 561. [7] GOR 82, 22 March 1955; SR 22, 15 April 1955. In the files of the AFMC History office; *Post-World War II Bombers*, pp. 560-561. [8] Letter, Brigadier General H. M. Estes, Jr. Director of Weapon Systems Operations, WADC, to the Commander ARDC, Subject: Chemically Powered Strategic Bomber Program, 7 April 1955; Letter, Major General G. H. Griswold, Vice Commander SAC to the Commander ARDC, Subject: System Requirement 22, 19 April 1955. In the files of the AFMC History Office. [9] Marcelle Size Knaack, *Post-World War II Fighters, 1945-1973*, (Washington DC: Office of Air Force History, 1986), p. 330. [10] *Post-World War II Bombers*, pp. 560-562. [11] *Post-World War II Fighters, 1945-1973*, p. 329. [12] Ibid, p. 329. [13] Ibid, p. 329. [14] Ibid, p. 330. [15] Ibid, p. 330. [16] Ibid, p. 331. [17] Boeing Report D2-2371, <u>Boeing Weapon System 110A</u>, December 1957; North American Report NA-56-825, <u>Strategic Bomber Weapon System 110A Summary Briefing</u>, 30 July 1956. [18] C.E. "Bud" Anderson, "Aircraft Wingtip Coupling Experiments," a paper prepared for the Society of Experimental Test Pilots, passim. [19] *Post-World War II Bombers*, p. 563. [20] Ibid, p. 563. [21] Ibid, p. 564. [22] Memorandum, T. H. Goss, Assistant Chief, 110A WSPO, to Chief, Power Plant Laboratory, WADC, Subject: Acceleration of System 110A/L Development, 26 March 1956. [23] Letter, Major General D. L. Putt, Deputy Chief of Staff for Development, to Commander ARDC, Subject: USAF Turbine Engine Development Program, 7 May 1957; TWX, RDTAP-5-7-E, Commander ARDC to Commander WADC, 17 May 1957. Both in the files of the AFMC History office. [24] *Post-World War II Bombers*, p. 564. [25] Ibid, pp. 564-566. [26] Alfred J. Eggers and Clarence A. Syverston, *Aircraft Configurations Developing High Lift/Drag Ratios at High Supersonic Speeds*, (Ames Research Center, CA: NACA, 5 March 1956), NACA research memorandum RM-A55105, passim. [27] *Post-World War II Bombers*, p. 566. [28] Ibid, p. 566. [29] Letter, E. A. Thomas, Acting Manager of Marketing, Jet Engine Division of General Electric, to Commander ARDC, Subject: WS-110A Programming, 13 January 1958; Memorandum, B-70 WSPO to DC/WS ARDC, Subject: Engine Interchangeability F-108/B-70, 3 July 1958; Letter, General E. W. Rawlings, Commander AMC to Deputy Chief of Staff for Materiel, no subject, 17 June 1958; Directive, Brigadier General B. H. Warren, Deputy Director for Procurement, to various AMC offices, Subject: B-70/F-108 Weapon Systems – J93 Engine Program, 12 September 1958. [30] *Post-World War II Bombers*, pp. 566-567.

A very late artist concept shows pretty much the final design. The canards appear to be on the large side, but this may have been artistic license. The vertical stabilizer size and the folding wingtips are approximately correct. (Gerald H. Balzer Collection)

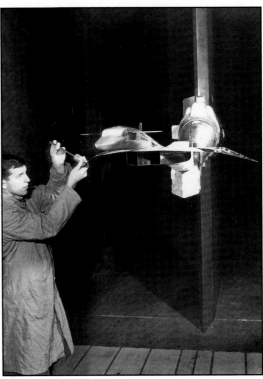

Not surprisingly, the B-70 spent a great deal of time in various wind tunnels. These are of a model at the NASA Ames Research Center. (NASA)

WARBIRD**TECH**
SERIES

TWO AIR 2 VEHICLES

The configuration chosen by North American was controversial given the long – and unsuccessful – history of canards on modern aircraft. Nevertheless, North American believed the canard was beneficial because of its long moment arm forward of the center-of-gravity. All aircraft suffer some instability at transonic speeds as the center-of-pressure moves rearward. The movement could be countered by trimming with the elevons, but this would increase the angle-of-attack, resulting in higher drag and a decrease in range (or speed, or both). In the B-70 design, small flaps on the trailing edge of the canard could be used to counter the center-of-pressure shift without changing the angle-of-attack of the main wing. This allowed trimming without a penalty in range or speed.[1]

The canard also helped minimize the extreme nose-up attitude most delta-wing aircraft use on landing. The canard flap could be deflected downward 25 degrees – when the flap was lowered at low speed, the aircraft nose pitched up. This change was compensated for by moving the control column forward, drooping the elevons on the main wing. This allowed the elevons to act as trailing-edge flaps without subtracting from the basic wing lift. Thus the landing attitude was shallower and the lift-to-drag ratio higher – permitting landing speeds comparable to other large high-performance aircraft.[2]

The detractors pointed out that canard designs generally had pitch and directional stability issues at high angles-of-attack, plus various flow disturbances around the engine inlets and wing. North American engineers countered that unlike most designs – which used

The final XB-70 mockup in February 1959. By this time the mockup had incorporated all of the changes that occurred during development. Of interest is the small fairing on the wing trailing edge (at left) for a defensive avionics sensor. A mockup of the Alert Pod may be seen behind the left landing gear in the photo above. (The Boeing Company)

The cockpit section of A/V-1 being mated with the other sections of the forward fuselage on 6 February 1962. Note the hole at the right that will support the all-moving canard. (Tony Landis Collection)

the canards as a horizontal stabilizer – the canard on the B-70 was only a trimming device; pitch and roll control was exclusively the function of the elevons. As for flow disturbances, given the extreme distance between the canard and air intake (which was at least partially protected by the wing) the engineers believed this was a non-issue. Some 14,000 hours of wind tunnel time backed up this assumption.[3]

EVOLUTION

The first major configuration change came during the summer of 1958. The gross weight increased from 483,000 to 537,109 pounds mainly because one of the two planned weapons bays was converted into a

The titanium cockpit section of AV-1 under construction on 3 February 1962. The four large escape hatches show up well here. Note that the aft bulkhead behind the rear escape hatches is angled just like it would be to support ejection seats in production aircraft. (Tony Landis Collection)

fuel tank. As a result, the airframe structure, landing gear, and tires had to be strengthened. The extra fuel was added – largely – because it was becoming obvious that the high energy fuel program was not going to materialize, at least not in the short term. This would force the use of conventional JP-4 in the –3 engine, and the accompanying 10 percent range penalty. The lift-over-drag (L/D) ratio was significantly improved by a reduction in the wing and canard thickness ratios. The result of these changes was a range improvement of 500 nm (from 5,200 to 5,700 nm).[4]

By the end of 1958 more changes improved the range to 6,539 nm without increasing the gross weight of the aircraft from the previous 537,109 pounds. Among the modifications, the fold line of the wing tips was changed to 60 percent of the semispan instead of the original 80 percent, resulting in a folding surface roughly the size of a B-58 wing. This alteration improved directional stability to such an extent that the vertical stabilizer area could be reduced by half, significantly lowering drag.[5]

At the same time, a movable windshield and ramp, variable geometry inlet, and trimmable canard were also introduced. The conventional canopy originally proposed caused a

The forward fuselage (above) for A/V-1 was moved to the final assembly building on 31 March 1962, while the center fuselage (below) arrived the following day. Note the cutout in the extreme nose for the attack radars, which were never installed in the two air vehicles that were completed. (Tony Landis Collection)

great deal of drag during supersonic flight. Switching to a movable ramp that could be lowered during landing significantly reduced this, and still allowed the pilots sufficient visibility to operate the aircraft. The change to the canard resulted in the entire surface being infinitely positionable between zero and 6 degrees to provide high-speed trim. Previously trim had been provided by moving the trailing edge flap. The flap now had

By 22 April 1962, the "neck" of A/V-1 was fairly well structurally complete. (Tony Landis Collection)

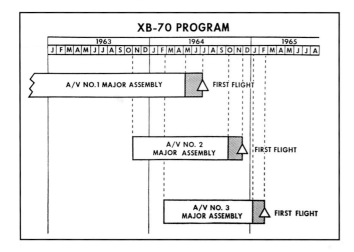

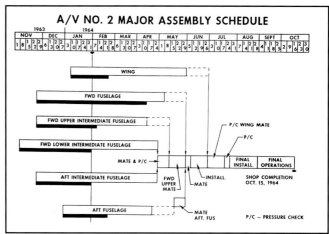

Two schedules for the XB-70 program. The one on the left shows the original assembly dates for the three air vehicles – in reality, A/V-2 was about 3 months months behind what is shown, and A/V-2 was six months delayed. A/V-3 was cancelled shortly after this schedule was presented. The schedule on the right shows the basic order the major components of each aircraft were manufactured and assembled in. (North American Aviation)

just two positions – zero and 20 degrees down – a change from its previous 25 degree maximum.* The wing area increased slightly from 6,100 to 6,297.15 square feet, and the outer leading edge was also twisted to reduce transonic drag. Increased turbine inlet temperatures in the J93 engines allowed a slightly reduced fuel flow during supersonic cruise.

Around the same time, the F-108 mockup was inspected on 26 January 1959, with few necessary changes identified. The aircraft was named Rapier on 15 May 1959, and first flight was expected in March 1961. The Air Force had a stated requirement for 480 of the aircraft.[6]

The B-70 development engineering inspection (DEI) was conducted at North American's Inglewood, California, plant on 2 March 1959, and the mockup was reviewed on 30 March 1959. The DEI provided the Air Force with a detailed analysis and theory of operation for each of the B-70 subsystems, while the mock-up review was oriented towards operational characteristics and suitability of the aircraft configuration.[7]

The Air Force issued 761 requests for alterations during the two reviews. One of the most significant was an order to incorporate provisions for the B-70 to carry air-to-surface missiles and provisions for external fuel tanks, a change that cost 17,500 pounds (including the missiles). No specific information could be ascertained about the missile (probably the GAM-87[†] Skybolt), but its inclusion can be found in the fact that the IBM offensive system was now officially called the "bombing-navigation, and missile guidance subsystem."

In order to keep the gross weight constant, North American deleted fuel, causing the projected range to decrease to 6,327 nm. The Air Force directed North American to recoup the lost range without increasing the gross weight beyond 554,609 pounds. Various minor changes were made and the range estimate increased to 6,500 nm when the missiles and external tanks were not installed. One aerial refueling extended the total range to 7,901 nm, permitting effective coverage of 96 percent of the desired targets.[8]

NEW SETBACKS

During January 1959 the engine program was ordered reevaluated – yet again. This review gave Pratt & Whitney a "slight edge" in various managerial and contractual factors. On the other hand, the General Electric engine rated higher in most technical areas. In addition General Electric had already accomplished full-scale afterburner testing with high-energy fuel. The J58 scored points for its relative mechanical simplicity and predicted easier production. The evaluation found both engines technically suitable, concluding that the differences between them were so minor as to preclude selecting one over the other "from a technical standpoint."[9]

There was one significant mechanical consideration, however. The

---

* Since the entire canard could deflect 6 degrees, plus another 20 degrees for the flap, the effective deflection was 26 degrees.
† The Douglas GAM-87 Skybolt was an air-launched ballistic missile that would have been carried on the B-52H and B-70A. Armed with a W59 nuclear warhead in a Mk. 7 re-entry vehicle, development was initiated in the late 1950s. The decision to proceed with the Skybolt was made in February 1960, with initial deployment projected for 1964. In June of 1960, the Royal Air Force ordered 100 Skybolts to be carried by the Avro Vulcan. However, in December of 1962, President Kennedy cancelled the Skybolt missile for political and economical reasons.

cruise performance of the aircraft depended on the efficiency of the convergent-divergent exhaust nozzle, and small differences could produce disproportionate variations in the aircraft's range. General Electric had already proved, on the J79, a mechanically-actuated nozzle that was similar to that for the J93; on the other hand, the aerodynamically-controlled nozzle Pratt & Whitney was developing for the J58 had not been tested and therefore carried some amount of development risk.[10]

In the end, it was decided to proceed with the J93 as the only engine for the two North American aircraft. Nevertheless, although it was technically a Navy program, the J58 would go on to power the CIA and Air Force Lockheed Blackbirds.

Decisions made in the second half of 1959 hampered several Air Force development efforts, but seemed to impact the B-70 more so than most.* As expected, the Department of Defense cancelled the high-energy fuel program on 10 August 1959. As a consequence, the J93-GE-5 engine destined for the B-70 was also cancelled since an engine without fuel is not terribly useful.[11]

As of 10 July 1959, the ill-fated –5 high energy fuel afterburner had been tested for 3 hours and 10 minutes at the Peebles Proving Ground in Ohio. The Arnold Engineering Development Center and the NASA Lewis Research Center had also conducted 3 hours and 1.5 hours of testing, respectively. In addition, there

had been five flights using high-energy fuel in the afterburner of a modified J57 engine on an F-101A.

The cancellation of the –5 engine and its exotic fuel caused a great

deal of concern within the B-70 program, but had little real impact. The fuel had been counted upon to provide the intercontinental range required for the primary strike mission. But the incorporation of fuel

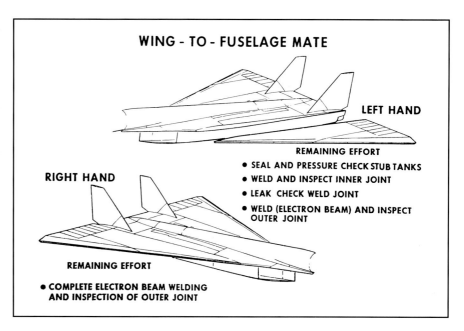

The wings on the B-70 were large – consider that the folding outer panel was about the size of a B-58 wing. The wing-to-fuselage joint was 80 feet long (the other 37 feet of chord was made up of fairings and elevons) and both the lower and upper surface of each honeycomb skin had to be welded. (Randy Cannon Collection)

The aft fuselage shows the location for the six J93 engines. This piece of the fuselage presented a challenge for the structural engineers – it needed to absorb the wing bending moments while providing large doors on the bottom for access to the engines. (Gerald H. Balzer Collection)

---

* The nuclear-powered bomber, after overshadowing the chemically-powered aircraft for years, began to suffer from financial malnutrition in 1956. By mid-1959, decisions within the Administration and Department of Defense had put the program into almost total eclipse. The project's downfall was bound to impede the B-70 program since the cost of several B-70 subsystems were to be developed by the nuclear-powered bomber program, which was finally cancelled by the Kennedy Administration in March 1961.

The first step in the Avcoramic Tooling process for fabricating the stainless steel honeycomb structures was the construction of a master model. Here, technicians at Avco's Aerospace Structures Division are placing a panel lay-up frame on the completed master model of the XB-70A upper forward intermediate fuselage section. (AVCO Corporation via the Gerald H. Balzer Collection)

tanks in the second weapons bay and increased aerodynamic efficiency had already provided a significant range boost to the B-70 design. At the same time, the petroleum industry had developed a new fuel – JP-6 – that offered significant efficiency improvements over JP-4, but was essentially interchangeable with the old fuel from an engine technology perspective. Unlike the boron-based fuels, JP-6 did not require special metals in the engine or fuel system. It was no worse environmentally than standard jet fuel, and was perhaps a bit better since it burned more completely.

Analysis showed that the –3 engine burning JP-6 could provide essentially the same range as had been expected with the –5 engine burning HEF-3. There were some compromises, however. The engine produced slightly less thrust, meaning takeoff distances would increase and refueling altitudes would be a little lower.

The most critical item – the rate of climb on a hot day with one engine inoperative at takeoff – was resolved by incorporating an overspeed capability into the –3 engine to develop a higher turbine inlet temperature on takeoff and thereby provide the necessary higher rate of climb.

Worse than the high energy fuel cancellation, on 24 September 1959 the F-108 was cancelled. The F-108 had used many of the same subsystems and technologies as the B-70 – the J93 engine program was managed and partially funded by the F-108 program, as were the escape capsules and several lesser subsystems. The loss of the second funding source would impact B-70 cost estimates by at least $180 million.[12]

ON THE ROPES

In early November 1959 President Dwight D. Eisenhower told the Air Force Chief of Staff that the "B-70 left him cold in terms of making military sense." Hardly impressed with the many pro-B-70 arguments put forth by General White, the President stressed that at anticipated funding levels the B-70 would not be operationally available for 8 to 10 years. By that time the major strategic retaliatory weapon would be the ICBM. The President finally agreed to take another look at the B-70, but pointed out that speaking of manned bombers in the missile age was like talking about bows and arrows in the era of gunpowder.[13]

Apparently the B-70 program still did not make sense to Eisenhower after another look. On 1 December 1959 the Air Force announced that the B-70 program would be reduced to a single prototype and that the development of most subsystems would be cancelled. The notable exception was that the advanced IBM bomb-nav system would continue to be developed as a very modest effort. The program's near-demise was generally attributed to the budget, although it was more directly linked to the Administration's anti-bomber sentiment that was prevalent at the time.[14]

However, the politics of the 1960 presidential campaign sparked renewed interest in the B-70 from both political parties. Thus, with the approval of the Department of Defense, in August 1960 the Air Force directed that the XB-70 prototype effort be changed once again to a full-scale development program. A letter contract (AF33(600)-42058) for the YB-70 weapon system was signed on 1 August to provide a single XB-70 prototype, 11 YB-70 service test aircraft, and to demonstrate the bomber's combat capability. This directive, coupled with a congressional appropriation of $265 million

for FY61, seemed to restore the B-70 to the status of a weapon system headed for production.[15]

In September 1960 North American was instructed to proceed with the design and manufacture of the 12 aircraft and to restart the development of all major subsystems. In mid-October the defensive subsystem contract with Westinghouse was reinstated, and in November the contract with Motorola for the mission and traffic control system was reactivated. The Air Force and North American also brought the IBM offensive avionics contract back up to a fully funded development effort. Unfortunately, the B-70 program's recaptured importance was to be short-lived.[16]

THREE STRIKES ...

Once in office, it did not take long for President John F. Kennedy to take a critical look at the B-70 program. Like his predecessor, Kennedy doubted the aircraft's reason for being, in no small part because the new Secretary of Defense Robert S. McNamara did not support any manned bomber program. On 28 March 1961, Kennedy recommended that the program be reoriented to exploring the problems of flying at three times the speed of sound with an aircraft "potentially useful" as a bomber. Kennedy underscored that this should only require the development of a small number of YB-70s and the continued development of the IBM bomb-nav system.[17]

Kennedy's words gave the Air Force no choice but to again redirect the B-70 program to a prototype development effort. The change became official on 31 March 1961 when North American was ordered to produce only three XB-70 prototypes.[18]

The forward intermediate fuselage section was manufactured by the AVCO Aerospace Structures Division in Nashville, Tennessee. After the fabrication and inspection of the various panels, they were joined by fusion welding. An AVCO technician is inspecting (above) the forward half of the section after the welding operation and before joining it with the aft half. The assembly was then fitted with stainless steel frames and bulkheads (below). It was subsequently packed and shipped to Palmdale. (AVCO Corporation via the Gerald H. Balzer Collection)

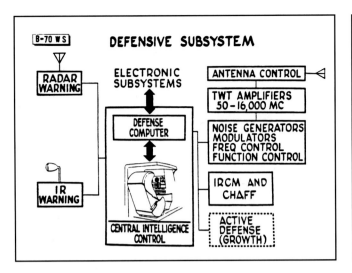

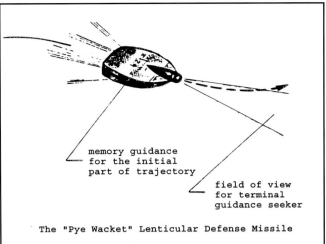

A functional schematic of the proposed YB-70 defensive avionics shows active jammers, infrared countermeasures, and chaff, along with radar and infrared warning systems. The box labeled "active defense" implied carrying air-to-air missiles. (U.S. Air Force)

One of the rather fanciful "active defense" systems considered for the YB-70 was this lenticular missile. Other ideas progressed further, including a defensive missile that eventually became the GAR-1 Falcon used on several Air Force interceptors. (U.S. Air Force)

Air Vehicle No. 1 (A/V-1)* was assigned the serial number (62-0001) originally allocated to the single XB-70 prototype under the December 1959 restructured program. The two additional aircraft were assigned serial numbers 62-0207 (A/V-2) and 62-0208 (AV/3). There is no record that the 11 YB-70s were ever allocated serials numbers.†

According to some sources, the third air vehicle was to be designated XB-70B; others called it a YB-70A which is more likely. This vehicle would have incorporated all of the improvements from A/V-2, and was to have been equipped with a prototype IBM bombing-navigation system and operable weapons bay in order to demonstrate its military mission. A crew of four would have been accommodated in the forward fuselage, with the defensive systems operator sitting behind the pilot and the offensive systems operator sitting behind the copilot, each in their own ejection capsules. As far as can be determined, the defense operator would have had

no equipment to operate since the defensive avionics program had been cancelled. It appears that the canard would also have been slightly reshaped to minimize drag. The hydraulic, electrical, and environmental control systems would all have required substantial changes to support the additional crew and electronics to be carried by AV/3.[19]

As a consequence of the latest restructuring, the General Electric engine program was also substantially reduced. The qualification tests for an operational "J" engine were eliminated leaving only the preliminary flight rating test for an experimental "XJ" power plant. Instead of continuing to refine the design and reducing weight wherever possible, which would increase development costs, General Electric was allocated an extra 150 pounds per engine over the weight specified for an operational power plant. A plan to use a B-58 test bed in the B-70 development program also disappeared, although it would later return.

Since it now appeared very unlikely that the B-70 would ever enter production, the Air Force immediately began to consider various alternatives. In May 1961 there was talk of an improved B-58 armed with air-launched missiles; specially-built, long-endurance, missile-launching aircraft; transport aircraft modified to launch ballistic missiles; resurrected nuclear-powered aircraft; and again of a reconnaissance B-70 that would also be capable of strike missions. In August, the U.S. Senate attempted once again to rescue the B-70 and asked that a production program be outlined to introduce the aircraft into the operational inventory at the earliest possible date. Undaunted, McNamara expressed his thorough dissatisfaction with any future manned bombers and refused to provide the data.[20]

---

* The two XB-70s were represented by various monikers during their test series: A/V-1, AV/1, and XB-70-1 all represented the first aircraft, while A/V-2, AV/2, and XB-70-2 represented the second. For consistency, this publication will use the A/V-x form.
† The 1,575 serial numbers beginning immediately after A/V-3 were assigned to the GAM-83A (AGM-12B) Bullpup.
‡ Some documentation refers to this as the RSB-70. Neither designation was truly official, but RS-70 seems more likely.

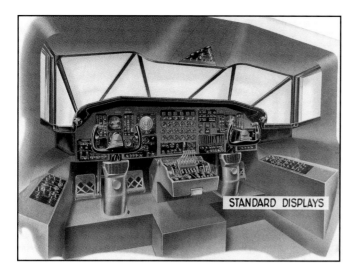
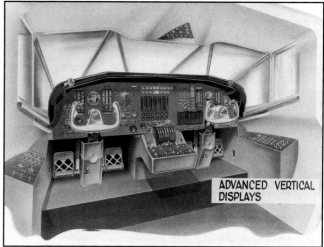

The artist concept at left shows the expected production cockpit using conventional instrumentation; it is conceptually similar to the cockpits installed on A/V-1 and A/V-2. The drawing at right shows a cockpit using vertical tape instruments for the engine displays. Interestingly, the center consoles changed a great deal also. (Jim Tuttle Collection)

In March 1962 Congress directed the Air Force to begin planning for a reconnaissance-strike version of the B-70, usually referred to as the RS-70.‡ In April, a group headed by General Bernard A. Schriever, Commander of the Air Force Systems Command, developed several approaches to the proposed RS-70 system. The preferred development plan would cost $1,600 million and estimated that the first RS-70 flight could occur within

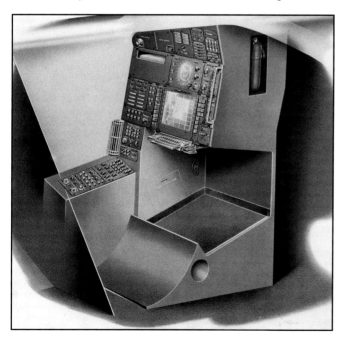

The defensive station (left) and offensive station (right) as they would have appeared on production B-70s. Although not often discussed, going to a four-man crew (in a heavy bomber) was an advanced concept for the era, although the B-58 medium bomber had made-do with only three men. The B-70 would have been fitted with a state-of-the-art defensive suite — unfortunately, nobody knew quite what it would look like. Initial consideration of adapting the ALQ-27 jamming system being developed (unsuccessfully, as it turned out) for the "improved" B-52 to the B-70 fell by the wayside when the configuration differences of the aircraft made the modifications impossible. The offensive avionics fared better, with IBM actually completing a prototype ASQ-28 bomb-nav system for A/V-3 prior to that aircraft's cancellation. The IBM system had been extensively test-flown on a variety of surrogate aircraft, although never as a complete package. (Jim Tuttle Collection)

The partially-completed AV-1 is moved from one part of the Palmdale facility to another for final work. Note that the forward fuselage has already received its white paint, and that all four escape hatches are missing. The vertical stabilizer stubs are in place – the rudders will be installed later, along with the wings and the rest of the skin on the upper fuselage. (Tony Landis Collection)

two years. Although the RS-70 concept languished for some time, ultimately the idea faded as Robert McNamara refused to release the funds Congress had authorized. Any dreams of production Valkyries vanished.[21]

GETTING READY

In reality, the construction of the two XB-70As went remarkably smoothly given how far they were pushing the state-of-the-art. Not unexpectedly, there were numerous small problems that the engineers and technicians had to overcome on an almost daily basis. But two major problems soon cropped up. The first involved manufacturing and assembling the stainless steel honeycomb panels. The problems encountered while manufacturing the first vehicle would eventually show up in flight tests when various pieces of skin routinely separated from A/V-1 at high speed.

The early 1960s saw the appearance of two Mach 3 aircraft in the United States – the XB-70A and the Lockheed Blackbirds. Each used a highly unique approach to development of an airframe capable of withstanding the temperatures created during high-speed flight. Lockheed decided to manufacture the Blackbirds almost exclusively of titanium alloys, and to accept a relatively hot structure and its implications. North American chose a different approach. Or perhaps the approach was forced upon them by the Air Force – available documentation does not give much insight into the process. It is known that the amount of high-grade titanium available to the industry at the time was very limited as was the production capacity (rolling, milling, etc.). The Blackbird was never envisioned (except, perhaps, in Kelly

Johnson's mind) as a large-scale production project, so the use of a relatively scarce resource was not much of an issue. However, the Air Force would have liked to build a large fleet of B-70s, and each aircraft would have required a significant amount of the material. It is very possible that the Air Force "suggested" that North American find a less strategic material for their construction. The source selection did note that Boeing had preferred titanium, but it is not known if this detracted from their score.

A/V-1 being repositioned at Palmdale. The wings have not been attached yet, but the rudders and the No. 4 engine have been installed. (Gerald H. Balzer Collection)

A/V-2 under construction. Note the drag chute compartment with one of the two doors installed. Plywood covers most of the upper wing area to prevent damage from people walking on the stainless steel honeycomb skin. The rudders have been installed and their white paint contrasts with the bare metal of the fixed portion of the vertical stabilizer. (Tony Landis Collection)

The dry weight of the XB-70A airframe was approximately 150,000 pounds, a little more than a fully-loaded Blackbird. The material North American chose for almost 69 percent of this was a PH15-7-Mo stainless steel honeycomb sandwich. Each XB-70A used approximately 20,000 square feet of the material. The attributes listed by North American were light weight, high strength, aerodynamic smoothness, low heat transfer from the skin to underlying structures at 450-640 degF, reliable strength at high temperatures, fatigue resistance, and rigidity. Producibility and relatively low cost were initially thought to be attributes, but these ended up to be very questionable as the program began procuring large amounts of the material.[22]

At least initially the material suffered from some serious problems. On numerous occasions pieces of the skin – sometimes large pieces – separated from the aircraft at high speeds. The worst was when A/V-1 lost a triangular section of its wing apex forward of its splitter plate and the debris was sucked into the air intakes, effectively destroying six engines. A/V-1 later lost a 40x36-inch piece from the underside of its left wing, and an 8x38-inch strip from its right fuselage section later still. The skin panels separated when thermal expansion and aerodynamic buffeting ballooned a defective area where the face sheet had cracked. This in turn led to the skin cover separating where the brazings were too thin or poorly formed. Engineers traced the immediate problem to flaws in the manufacturing process. Better quality control was implemented. When a void was detected, it was repaired by welding pins between the outer and inner face sheets, through the honeycomb structure. Along with improved fabrication techniques, this essentially eliminated the problem in A/V-2 although a large piece did separate from the upper surface of its right wing during one high-speed flight. North American was sure that the process would eventually be perfected, and the Air Force did not appear overly worried. Still,

A good look at the wing fold hinge before the aerodynamic fairing is added. The power hinge was a very robust structure given that the folding part of each wing was about the same size as a B-58 wing. Production models may have carried fuel in the folding section, further stressing this area. (Gerald H. Balzer Collection)

it is an open question if the material would have been satisfactory in large-scale use.

Although not the primary construction material, three types of titanium nevertheless accounted for approximately 12,000 pounds (8 percent) of the airframe in 22,000 individual parts. An alloy called 6Al-4V was used in thickness of 0.030 to 0.070-inch for the skin of the forward 60-feet of the fuselage where temperatures were expected to be 450–550 degF. The second alloy was 4Al-3Mo-1V, used primarily for the internal structure of the forward fuselage. The third was 7Al-4Mo , used for various forgings and extrusions. Sheet titanium represented 50 percent of the total; 25 percent was plate 0.75 to 1-inch thick; and the remainder was in the form of forgings and extrusions. A limited amount of René-41 was also used in the engine compartment because of its very high temperature qualities.[23]

The other major problem was fuel tank sealing. Based largely on the initial requirement to use boron fuels, the fuel tanks were designed to be pressurized and purged by gaseous nitrogen, and the design criteria said that the tanks had to withstand 10 psi with no leakage. However, when A/V-1 was first tested, the fuel tanks leaked – a lot. The majority of the leaks were caused by pin-hole flaws where the tanks had been welded during construction. Brazing repairs to the leaking areas proved ineffective. After various trials and errors, North American decided to coat the inside of the tanks using du Pont Viton-B as a sealant. A single coat of Viton-B was painted on and then cured for six hours while being heated to 375 degF by electric blankets (or even hair dryers in some inaccessible

A/V-2 under construction in Palmdale. Although she was largely constructed of stainless steel honeycomb, enough titanium was used to cause North American many of the same difficulties experienced by Lockheed while building the Blackbirds. (The Boeing Company)

A nearly completed A/V-2 shows its outer wing panel and undersurface detail. Note the large jack-stands holding the aircraft up. Two of the elevons have not been installed yet and the engine compartment is empty. As on most aircraft, the rudders were painted prior to installation since they need to be balanced as they are installed, and the weight of the paint affects this process. (Tony Landis Collection)

areas). The process was repeated up to six times on each tank. The tanks were then pressurized with helium and a "sniffer" used to detect leaks. The process worked, except on tank No. 5 in A/V-1. This U-shaped tank at the extreme rear of the fuselage was considered too small and too inaccessible to warrant the time necessary to properly correct the leaks so the fuel pumps were removed and the tank made inoperative.[24]

It should be noted that the Viton-B solution was not considered satisfactory for production aircraft – engineers estimated it would have a useful life of only 1,000 hours before it would need to be stripped off and reapplied. However, since the B-70 flight test program was scheduled to last only 180 flight hours, it was considered adequate. The welds on A/V-2 were subjected to better quality control and the fuel system exhibited significantly fewer leaks.

The vertical stabilizers are fitted to A/V-1 (above) and the airframe is rolled out of the hanger to be repositioned (below) still minus the wings. Notice that the serial number has not been painted on yet. (Gerald H. Balzer Collection)

[1] Iain Pike, B-70 State-of-the-Art Improver, *Flight International*, 25 June 1964, p. 1059. [2] Ibid, p. 1059. [3] Ibid, p. 1059. [4] North American Report NAA-58-984, Estimated performance Record for the B-70 Air Vehicle Powered with Six (6) General Electric J-93 Turbojet Engines, 15 August 1958. [5] North American Report NA-59-268, Estimated Performance and Drag Substantiation Report for B-70 Primary Air Vehicle, 27 February 1959. [6] Marcelle Size Knaack, *Post-World War II Fighters, 1945-1973*, (Washington DC: Office of Air Force History, 1986), p. 331. [7] Marcelle Size Knaack, *Post-World War II Bombers*, (Washington DC: Office of Air Force History, 1988), p. 567. [8] Letter, Harrison A. Storms, Chief Engineer, North American Aviation, to Commander AMC, Subject: Contract AF33(600)-38669, B-70 Weapon System Configuration Status, 15 May 1959; Letter, Harrison A. Storms to Commander AMC, Subject: B-70 Weapon System Configuration Review, 12 June 1959; North American Report NA-59LA-3927A, Configuration Analysis, 3 March 1959. [9] Letter, Colonel J. R. V. Dickson, Assistant Director for Research and Development, USAF, to Commander ARDC, no subject, 29 December 1958. [10] Ibid. [11] *Post-World War II Bombers*, p. 567. [12] Ibid, p. 567. [13] Ibid, p. 568. [14] Ibid, p. 568. [15] North American Rockwell Report SD-72-SH-0003, B-70 Aircraft Study, Final Report, Volume I, April 1972, prepared under NASA contract NAS9-12100, p. 31; *Post-World War II Bombers*, p. 568. [16] Ibid, pp. 568-569. [17] Ibid, p. 569. [18] North American Rockwell Report SD-72-SH-0003, B-70 Aircraft Study, Final Report, Volume I, April 1972, prepared under NASA contract NAS9-12100, p. 31. [19] "XB-70A 's Research Role will Contribute Mach 3 Flight Data for SST Development," *Aviation Week & Space Technology*, 18 May 1964, pp. 26-27. [20] *Post-World War II Bombers*, pp. 569-570. [21] North American Rockwell Report SD-72-SH-0003, B-70 Aircraft Study, Final Report, Volume I, April 1972, prepared under NASA contract NAS9-12100, p. 31; *Post-World War II Bombers*, p. 570. [22] B-70 State-of-the-Art Improver, p. 1060. [23] "XB-70A 's Research Role will Contribute Mach 3 Flight Data for SST Development," *Aviation Week & Space Technology*, 18 May 1964, pp. 26-27; B-70 State-of-the-Art Improver, p. 1060. [24] B-70 State-of-the-Art Improver, p. 21.

A good view of A/V-2 under construction in December 1964. Note the missing upper wing skin on the right. At this point the aircraft was six months away from being rolled out. (Tony Landis Collection)

The summer before first flight was spent conducting many tests. Here the outer wing panels on A/V-1 are moved to their mid- (left) and full-down (right) positions. The aircraft is sitting on tall jackstands since the wing panels would not clear the ground while the aircraft was on its landing gear. Engineers and technicians are gathered around the power hinge, checking to make sure everything worked the way they had planned. (Tony Landis Collection)

The main landing gear on A/V-1 during vibration testing. The only part of the door structure that remained open when the gear was down was the small piece shown here. (Gerald H. Balzer Collection)

7-26-62 278-7-212 DD

The No. 4 engine is installed into A/V-1 on 26 July 1962 for a functional check. The J93 was a very large engine for the day, but remarkably, with a little practice technicians could swap one out in less than half an hour. Note that one rudder has been installed, but the other has not. (Tony Landis Collection)

As with most significant military developments during the Cold War, the XB-70A was matched by a Soviet counterpart. In this case it was the Sukhoi T-4 (also called Project 100). This titanium and stainless steel aircraft was powered by four 35,274-lbf Kolesov RD36-41 turbojet engines and was designed to reach Mach 3. The development program was cancelled before the aircraft ever flew that fast. Like the B-70, the T-4 had an articulating nose, but in the up position all forward vision was lost. (above left: Jay Miller; below: Drawn by Tony Landis; others: Jay Miller Collection)

Sukhoi T-4

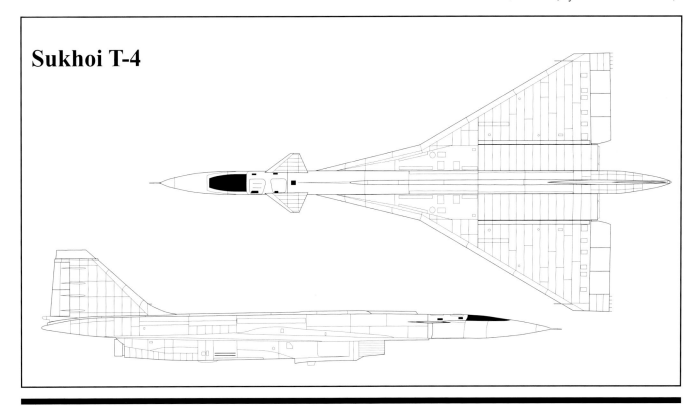

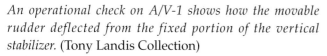

An operational check on A/V-1 shows how the movable rudder deflected from the fixed portion of the vertical stabilizer. (Tony Landis Collection)

North American toyed with SSTs that used the basic B-70 shape, as evidenced by these staged photos. (top: Gerald H. Balzer Collection; above: Tom Rosquin Collection)

Early morning before the roll-out of A/V-1 … making sure everything is ready. (Tony Landis Collection)

WARBIRD**TECH**
S E R I E S

A SHEEP IN WOLF'S CLOTHING

The two XB-70As were assembled in a new facility on the north side of Air Force Plant No. 42 in Palmdale, California, although almost all of the major sections were manufactured elsewhere. A/V-1 was rolled out of the hanger on a slightly overcast Monday, 11 May 1964. Just sitting on the ground, the Valkyrie awed the audience – her sleek lines left no doubt she was designed for speed. But just two months later, continuing fiscal problems forced the elimination of the partially-built AV/3 and the reduction the flight test program to only 180 hours – hardly enough to really justify the expense of the two remaining vehicles. The flight program was to be run by the Air Force to gather data for military programs, but NASA had already signed-on to provide instrumentation for a number of SST-related experiments. It was hoped that the Air Force program would be sufficiently successful to justify a follow-on program that would probably be run by NASA and aimed more directly at SST research.[1]

The four months following roll-out were spent performing the tests that are always done on first-of-a-type vehicles – including low- and high-speed taxi tests on Palmdale's long runway, plus engine runs and fuel system tests.

On 21 September 1964, A/V-1 was ready for its first flight. As initially planned, the 1.75-hour hop would be rather spectacular for a maiden flight. Since Plant 42 was in a populated area (sort of), caution would be exercised immediately after takeoff – the landing gear would remain down and the airspeed low. But once the Valkyrie was over Edwards AFB, the plan called for retracting the landing gear and accelerating through the speed of sound at 30,000 feet. If the aircraft went supersonic on the first flight, North American would receive a $250,000 bonus from the Air Force.[2]

Before sunrise Alvin S. White, North American Chief Test Pilot, and Colonel Joseph E. Cotton, Air Force B-70 Chief Test Pilot, began the preflight inspection, although the ground crew had checked the aircraft so carefully that there was little chance that anything had been overlooked.

At 06:10, White and Cotton climbed aboard the Valkyrie to begin the preflight checklist. Engine No. 1 was started and brought up to operating temperature 35 minutes later. In the process of starting the second J93, however, caution lights indicated a failure in the engine's cooling loop. Both engines were shut down. A few minutes later, the problem was traced to a tripped circuit breaker.

The process of starting the engines began again at 07:14. With 132,000 pounds (more than the weight of a Blackbird) of fuel in the tanks, A/V-1 began taxiing towards the Palmdale main runway. Earlier taxi tests had revealed a brake chatter during low-speed operations, so White and Cotton exercised caution

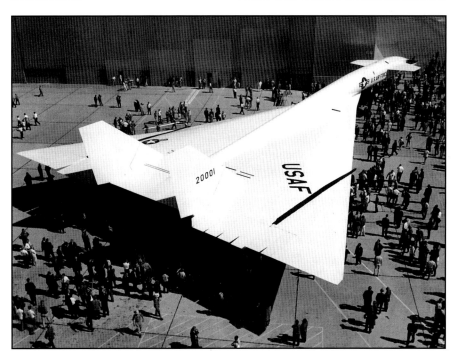

The traditional roll-out photo of A/V-1 shows the large area provided by the delta wing and the general size of the vehicle compared to the people milling around it. (North American)

– the demonstrated braking distance from just 5 mph was 400 feet. After what must have seemed an interminable taxi, the XB-70A arrived at the end of the runway. Every journey begins but with a single step.

At 08:24 Al White advanced the six throttles to maximum afterburner, rotating to 9 degrees angle-of-attack at 193 knots. After using 4,853 feet of runway, at 205 knots the 387,620-pound Valkyrie became airborne for

the first time. Three chase aircraft accompanied the XB-70A – a single B-58 and two T-38s. Two HH-21 helicopters also were airborne as crash-rescue vehicles during takeoff in Palmdale. Per the flight plan, speed was held at 310 knots and the gear left down for the flight to Edwards. No unusual handling problems occurred during this time. A second pair of T-38s replaced the first two when their fuel ran low.[3]

The rollout of A/V-1 on 11 May 1964 at Air Force Plant 42 in Palmdale, California. (above: North American Aviation via the Gerald H. Balzer Collection; below: AFFTC History Office Collection)

The trip to Edwards was relatively short, even at only 310 knots. Per the flight plan, while over Rogers Dry Lake , Joe Cotton retracted the landing gear – or at least attempted to. A minute later a chase plane called out that the retraction sequence had failed. In order to fit into the fuselage, the main landing gear used a complex series of motions. From an extended point, the bogie rotated 90 degrees to become perpendicular to

WARBIRD**TECH**
S E R I E S

the normal direction of travel. Then the bogie rotated 90 degrees vertically so that rear set of wheels were almost touching the top of the main strut. At this point, the main gear folded rearward into the gear well. It had been successfully demonstrated in both the test rig and on A/V-1 many times.

This time, however, the right side gear had stopped after only completing the first motion (rotating perpendicular to the direction of flight). A chase plane reported fluid was leaking onto the fuselage behind the gear doors – in mid-flight, the only thing to do was to fully extend the landing gear before a loss of hydraulic pressure made it impossible to do so. Cycled back to the extended position, the gear locked into place.

White and Cotton decided to use a pre-established alternate plan that called for a shorter flight at reduced speed with the gear extended. The flight lasted 1 hour and 7 minutes, reaching Mach 0.5 at just 16,000 feet. White and Cotton then proceeded to line up for landing on the 15,000-foot runway at Edwards. The pilot's position – almost 110 feet in front of the landing gear – combined with the nose-up attitude required to land the big delta, made it difficult for the pilots to judge their height above the runway. (It was not until the tenth

Before you can walk, you must learn to crawl. A/V-1 on her first taxi test 9 August 1964 at Palmdale. (AFFTC History Office Collection)

The first flight of A/V-1 from Palmdale on 21 September 1964. (AFFTC History Office Collection)

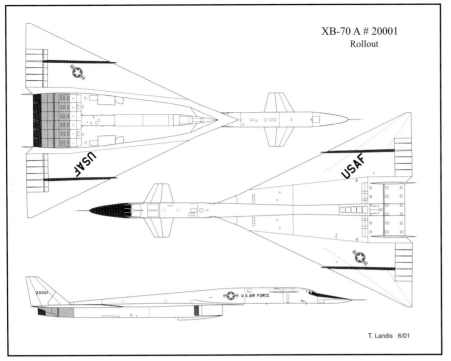

XB-70 A # 20001
Rollout

T. Landis 6/01

The aircraft remained on the runway for over eight hours while the aircraft was defueled and the landing gear was repaired.

In addition to the landing gear problems, the No. 3 engine had an overspeed indication soon after the landing gear failed to retract. White shut the engine down as a precaution after it registered 108 percent on the tachometer. Originally this was thought to be an instrumentation error, but further investigation discovered the engine did have a problem. To make matters worse, the No. 2 engine ingested debris while landing – both engines were replaced. Despite these mishaps, White and Cotton reported that the aircraft had flown well. But North

flight that Al White stopped using the chase planes to call out his altitude.) Nevertheless, Al White set the XB-70A safely on the ground 2,000 feet down Runway 04.

But the troubles were not over. As A/V-1 landed, the left main bogie failed to pivot (the rear wheels were designed to touch down first, then the bogie would pivot so that the front wheels touched down). This led to sparks and a minor fire during landing rollout. The XB-70A rolled for 10,800 feet before stopping, the Edwards crash team in hot pursuit.

The left main gear after the first flight. The bogie had not pivoted into the correct position prior to landing, leading to a minor fire on the runway at Edwards. The brake stack between the two aft wheels shows up well in the photo at left. (Tony Landis Collection)

American did not collect the quarter million dollar bonus.[4]

On 5 October 1964, White and Cotton took A/V-1 into the air again with the full intent of going supersonic. If they were successful on this flight, North American would receive a $125,000 bonus. However, if they failed North American would be assessed penalties (beginning at $125,000) for each additional flight until the XB-70A broke the sound barrier.

Following takeoff, with a chase plane on each side, the landing gear was retracted, then lowered, then retracted again without a problem. With the landing gear up and stowed, the XB-70A climbed to 28,000 feet and accelerated to Mach 0.85 (600 knots). A new problem – the No. 1 utility hydraulic system began losing pressure, and White headed back to Edwards. On the final approach, the landing gear had

XB-70 "Maiden Flight"

"I KNOW YOU ALWAYS TAKE AN EXTRA MEASURE OF PRECAUTION COLONEL COTTON, BUT:… "

Is a caption really necessary? (AFFTC History Office Collection)

to be lowered using the emergency electrical system. The actual touchdown on the lake bed was uneventful, and A/V-1 rolled to a stop after 10,000 feet, despite one of the main drag chutes refusing to deploy. No bonus for North American.

A week later, on 12 October 1964, A/V-1 accelerated through the sound barrier for the first time, reaching Mach 1.11 at 35,400 feet for 15 minutes before decelerating beneath the sound barrier and breaking back through several times

A/V-1 undergoing pre-flight checks prior to her second flight on 5 October 1964. At this point, the air vehicle still looked pristine in her glossy white paint. Note the amount of ground equipment surrounding the aircraft, and the collection of cars parked on the side of the taxiway. (AFFTC History Office Collection)

to check transonic stability. Again, one of the drag chutes opened late during landing, but did not seriously affect the rollout.

The fourth flight, on 24 October, fulfilling the Phase One test objectives of demonstrating the basic airworthiness of the aircraft. White and Cotton were again at the controls for a flight lasted that 1 hour and 25 minutes with A/V-1 reaching Mach 1.42 at 46,300 feet. For the first time,

the wingtips were lowered to their mid-down 25-degree position. The XB-70A remained supersonic for 40 minutes, establishing a new record for sustained supersonic flight.

The aircraft returned to Palmdale at the end of this flight for a series of structural tests. These tests would be non-destructive in nature since the program had not built a dedicated structural test airframe.[*] While at Palmdale, engineers puzzled over

why some of the glossy white paint peeled off during three of the first four flights. It was finally determined that too-thick paint caused by several re-paintings (in order to impress various VIPs) was being cracked as the Valkyrie flexed in flight, and was then torn away by the airstream. During her winter stay at Plant 42, A/V-1 was stripped and repainted with a single thin coat of white paint. A major exterior change was that the bottom fuselage around the engines was now painted white instead of being left natural titanium finish as it had been for the first four flights.

Looking worse for the wear – A/V-1 on the lakebed after her second flight on 5 October 1964. The gloss white paint has begun to peel off the canards, upper wings, and vertical stabilizers. A failure in the utility hydraulic system forced Al White and Joe Cotton to land on the lakebed as a precaution, although the actual landing was uneventful. (AFFTC History Office Collection)

Structural testing completed satisfactorily, Phase Two testing began on 16 February 1965, when Al White and Joe Cotton took the Valkyrie on its fifth flight. For the first time, the wingtips were lowered to the full 65-degree position, and A/V-1's manual air inlet control system (AICS) throat ramps were cycled. This flight lasted 1 hour and 10 minutes, including 40 minutes at Mach 1.6 and 45,000 feet. Continuing an unhappy trend, the drag chutes again failed to deploy completely, and A/V-1 required 11,100 feet to rollout.

The sixth flight, on 25 February 1965, marked the first time someone other than White and Cotton was at the controls. Lieutenant Colonel Fitzhugh "Fitz" Fulton (later to be NASA's chief test pilot) flew as copilot with Al White. But again, hydraulic leaks cut the flight short. Engineers at North American worked diligently to modify the hydraulic systems to end the constant leakage problems that had disrupted every flight. These changes were never totally effective on

_____
* A few "test specimens" had been built however, including most of an aft fuselage that was used for wing bending tests, loads in the duct region, and fuel tank verification.

The paint problem on the second flight got much worse on the third as A/V-1 pushed through the sound barrier for the first time. Yet more paint would come off during the fourth flight. The problem was that the paint was too thick, and peeled off as the airframe flexed. A/V-1 would be stripped and repainted before the fifth flight. (AFFTC History Office Collection)

Times were simpler, and the equipment less complex than today. Here is the North American mobile command center bus that was used to support the XB-70 program at Edwards. (AFFTC History Office Collection)

A/V-1, but greatly benefited A/V-2 during its construction.

On 4 March, the seventh flight had White and Fulton sustaining supersonic flight for 60 minutes, reaching a top speed of Mach 1.85 and 50,200 feet. North American's Van Shepard made his first flight as copilot during the eighth flight on 24 March 1965 reaching Mach 2.14 and 56,100 feet – 40 minutes were spent above Mach 2; another 34 minutes above Mach 1.

The 12th flight was on 7 May 1965, with White and Fulton at the controls. Travelling at Mach 2.60 (1,690 mph), a "thump" was heard in the cockpit, followed by multiple engine-related alarms – engines Nose. 3, 4, 5, and 6 were shut down as a precaution. As the chase planes caught up, they reported that the horizontal splitter (the apex of the delta wing) had torn away. The debris had been sucked into the intakes and done severe damage to the engines. For the final approach, the No. 5 engine was restarted to provide some thrust from the right side, and A/V-1 landed on the long lake bed without major incident. All six engines, nearly one-sixth of the 38 built, were considered damaged beyond repair. After this flight, the splitter itself was replaced with a single solid piece of titanium alloy in place of the honeycomb unit that had failed. At this point, concerns about the integrity of the honeycomb skin began, and the next four flights concerned themselves with "heat soaking" the skin for sustained periods of time. For the first time, the ability of the XB-70A to reach Mach 3 was seriously questioned.

Still, the program aimed higher and faster. On 1 July 1965, during her 14th flight, A/V-1 recorded Mach 2.85 at 68,000 feet for 10 minutes. On this flight, several sheets of honeycomb skin were lost from the fuselage and upper wing surface; fortunately no debris was ingested by the engines. Mach 3 was getting closer, but doubts persisted.

A/V-2 JOINS THE FRAY

Most of the major problems plaguing A/V-1 were cured on A/V-2, which was rolled out on 29 May 1965. In addition to having a functional No. 5 fuel tank, A/V-2 had 5-degrees of dihedral on the main wing, versus the zero degrees on

A/V-1 underwent a non-destructive structural test between the fourth and fifth flights. The tests were conducted at the North American facility in Palmdale. (Gerald H. Balzer Collection)

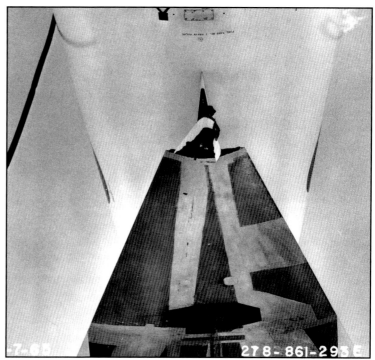

Not a good day. During the 12th flight on 7 May 1965 the horizontal splitter broke off of A/V-1 and was ingested by the engines. Although the aircraft landed without major incident, all six engines were beyond repair. (AFFTC History Office Collection)

Engine No. 4
Guide vanes - minor
Compressor blades - major
(see fig. 5(a))

ngine No. 6
uide Vanes - minor
ompressor blades - major
see Fig. 5(c))

Engine No. 5
Guide vanes and
blades -- major
(see fig. 5(b))

Fairing gashed by
leading component
of apex.

Rear gash in floor of duct.
(see fig. 4(c))

Forward gash in floor of duct.
(see fig. 4(b))

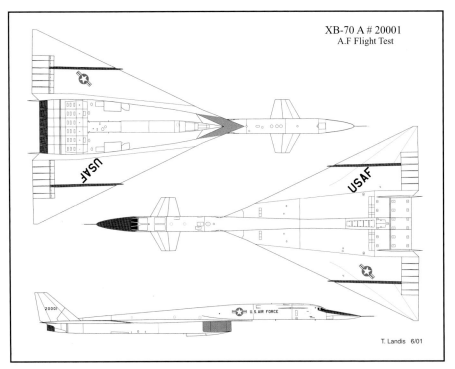

When A/V-1 emerged from her structural tests she sported a new paint job. The only major difference was that the lower fuselage around the engines was painted white, and the air intakes were in natural metal. (Drawn by Tony Landis)

A/V-1. This change was a result of wind tunnel testing that showed A/V-1 would have poor roll stability with the wingtips fully lowered. The tradeoff was that, at low speeds with the wingtips up, A/V-2 suffered from a "dihedral effect" where sideslip caused one wing to drop. The pilot, sensing the low wing but not spotting the sideslip, would use the elevons to bring the wing back up – causing more sideslip, forcing the wing to drop lower. The only solution was for the pilots to closely watch the sideslip indicator. It was expected that any production aircraft would cure this anomalous behavior with changes to the stability augmentation system.

Internally, A/V-2 featured a revised hydraulic system to reduce the leaking that continued to trouble A/V-1. The techniques to build the honeycomb skin also improved with experience, resulting in a stronger material that hopefully would not separate. An automatic control for the AICS was installed, in place of the manual system on the first aircraft. The most visible external difference was that the radome for the non-existent bomb-nav system was painted black on A/V-2; it was white on A/V-1.

The rollout of A/V-2 on 29 May 1965 The obvious external difference was the black radome under the nose; the wing dihedral, automated AICS, and improved fuel tanks were more subtle. (AFFTC History Office Collection)

On 17 July 1965 A/V-2 joined the flight test program. With much better luck than had accompanied A/V-1's first flight, the wingtips were lowered 65 degrees, and a top speed of Mach 1.41 at an altitude of 42,000 feet was reached before landing at Edwards AFB. The second flight of A/V-2 was significant in that it was the first time that Al White was not the pilot-in-command of an XB-70A – he and Joe Cotton swapped seats on 10 August 1965 while A/V-2 recorded Mach 1.45 at 41,000 feet.

Initially, A/V-2 was not completely trouble-free. Brake chatter continued to be a problem during low-speed taxiing; it was suspected that this stemmed from the lack of return springs for the brake pads. Far more troubling, however, were problems in the automatic AICS system, which would inexplicably recycle during supersonic flight, causing an "unstart."

The normal climb schedule for the XB-70A consisted of a series of accelerations, combined with variations in wingtip, windshield, and air inlet geometry. The landing gear was retracted early. Wingtips were lowered to mid-down anywhere from 400 knots to 630 knots to provide extra stability in the transonic region. Steady acceleration to Mach 1.5 at 32,000 feet followed, then the wingtips were lowered to their full-down position. Mach 1.5 was maintained to about 50,000 feet, and then varying rates of acceleration were applied until Mach 3 (2,000 mph) at 70,000 feet was reached. The best-recorded time to Mach 3 was 25 minutes from rotation.

From Mach 2 on, the rectangular air inlet ramps began to close. As speed increased, their geometry changed

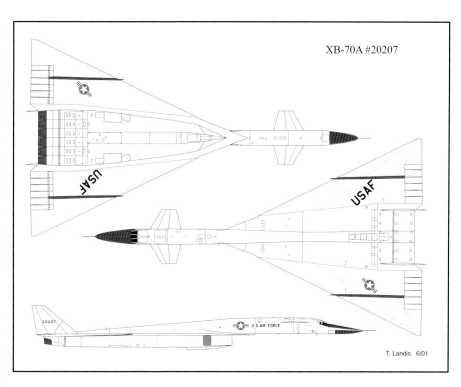

The black radome was the easiest way to identify A/V-2. (Drawn by Tony Landis)

to provide the optimum pressure recovery through a series of sequential shocks; beginning with an oblique shock from the splitter plate, ending with a terminal shock as the air reached the throat areas. Introducing the initial shock wave was "starting" the inlet ramps. If the shock wave refused to enter, or popped back out of the inlets, it was called an "unstart" condition.

Al White described an unstart at Mach 3 as sudden and violent, accompanied by a large reduction in engine thrust. The aircraft rolled, pitched, and yawed, accompanied by considerable buffeting. Normally one inlet unstarted with a bang and as the pilot was recovering the other inlet would unstart. Similar problems also affected the Lockheed Blackbirds – it was one of the haz-

The first flight of A/V-2 was on 17 July 1965, also from Palmdale. (AFFTC History Office Collection)

For reasons we will not explore here, a sack of Idaho potatoes were flown on the 14 October 1965 flight when A/V-1 exceeded Mach 3 for the first (and only) time. Note the markings on back of coveralls. The large box behind the people is part of the instrumentation that was carried in the weapons bay. (AFFTC History Office Collection)

ards of very high speed flight. While not particularly dangerous, unstarting was one problem facing supersonic transport designers. Passengers aboard an SST would not appreciate such an occurrence in flight. Nor would their stomachs.

There was another, potentially more serious problem. Sometimes, speed and throat ramp settings would create a condition where the shock wave was right at the boundary of the inlet, jumping in and out. This "buzz" had to be corrected quickly –

if it continued for more than a few minutes the stresses could cause structural damage.

Despite the problems, by its eighth flight A/V-2 had reached Mach 2.34 at 57,500 feet. However, Al White's post-flight report recommended waiting until the AICS was fixed before attempting Mach 3 flight.

ONWARD TO MACH 3

In the meantime A/V-1 continued to go faster. Finally, on 14 October 1965, A/V-1 recorded Mach 3.02 at 70,000 feet. As A/V-1 accelerated through Mach 3 Al White reported "There's that big magic number [Mach 3]." For just over two minutes everything appeared fine. Suddenly, White and Cotton heard something behind them. Although no caution lights had come on White decided to decelerate and let the chase planes catch up. They soon reported that about 2 feet of the left wing's leading edge was missing. Fortunately, the damaged section of the wing was far enough outboard that the debris wasn't drawn into the engine inlets.

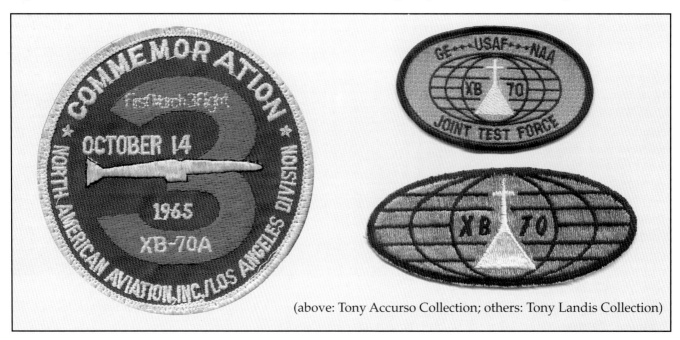

(above: Tony Accurso Collection; others: Tony Landis Collection)

After 56 weeks and 17 flights, A/V-1 had finally reached her goal – but she would never fly at Mach 3 again. Alarmed with the skin separation problems, and hoping that improvements in A/V-2 would solve the problem, the Air Force imposed a Mach 2.5 speed limitation on A/V-1. Still, for a while A/V-1 was the largest and heaviest aircraft to have ever flown Mach 3, even if only for two minutes.

During her 15th flight, on 11 December 1965, A/V-2 reached Mach 2.94 briefly, but ran at Mach 2.8 for 20 minutes (spending 41 total minutes above Mach 2.5) without any indications of skin separation. Ten days later, after 7 minutes above Mach 2.9 (and 32 minutes above Mach 2.8), the oil pump for the No. 4 engine failed. Shutting down the engine, White and Cotton headed back to Edwards, when an over temperature caution came on for the No. 6 engine, which was shut down as well. After landing, it was discovered that, despite the early shutdown, loss of lubrication had destroyed engine No. 4 – the flight program only had 29 engines remaining. The No. 6 engine was removed and sent to General Electric for repair.

Less than 6 months after her first flight, A/V-2 reached Mach 3 on her 17th flight – coincidentally, the same number of flights A/V-1 needed to reach Mach 3. A top speed of Mach 3.05 (2,010 mph) was recorded for 3 minutes, although 17 additional minutes had been spent above Mach 2 and 16 more above Mach 1. The post-flight inspection revealed no sign of skin damage. Prudence was still the watchword, however, and A/V-2 twice more poked her sleek nose beyond Mach 3 for just a few minutes before sustaining 2,000 mph

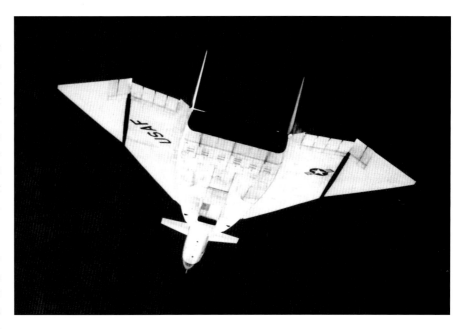

A/V-2 with the wingtips in the mid-down position. The two elevon segments on the outer wing panels were locked in the neutral position when the wingtips were folded. (Jay Miller Collection)

at 73,000 feet for 15 minutes during her 22nd flight on 17 February 1966.

The two aircraft seemed determined to add excitement at the same intervals. Both aircraft exceeded Mach 3 on their 17th flights. Each of their 37th flights added a different type of excitement.

On 7 March 1966 the 37th flight of A/V-1 showed the type of adversity that could be overcome by a pair of experienced test pilots. Van Shepard was the pilot and Joe Cotton was copilot. Halfway through the planned flight, both hydraulic systems began to fail. Shepard quickly brought the Valkyrie home as Cot-

The second Valkyrie taxis at Edwards. Note that the trailing edge flaps on the canard are in their lowered position. (Jay Miller Collection)

A/V-1 made an emergency landing on 7 March 1966 during A/V-1's 37th flight. Van Shepard was the pilot; Joe Cotton the co-pilot. Pete Hoag and Fitz Fulton were flying chase in an F-104. The landing gear problem forced an unusual three-mile J-shaped rollout on the lakebed. (above: Fitz Fulton Collection; others: Tony Landis Collection)

ton extended the landing gear. No green indicators came on, followed by a call from the chase plane that there was trouble with both sets of main gear. On the left side, the gear had not fully lowered before rotating to meet the direction of travel, leaving the rear wheels higher, rather than lower, than the front set of wheels.

The right side gear was in worse shape – it hadn't lowered at all before rotating. Even more alarming, it hadn't rotated completely in line with the direction of travel, although it was close. Neither the backup or emergency system corrected the problem. After what must have seemed like hours in the cockpit, engineers on the ground called up to the pilots with their plan. Shepard would land the Valkyrie on the dry lake bed, so there would be plenty of room. The engineers believed that, on touchdown, the left gear would

Van Shepard set A/V-1 down on the lake bed, and each main gear did what the engineers expected. The aircraft was down and rolling, but she wanted to turn sharply to the right – threatening to ground loop, which, although probably not fatal to the pilots, would likely destroy the aircraft. So Shepard kept applying power to the No. 6 (farthest right side) engine to help keep the XB-70A somewhat straight.

After rolling almost three miles, the XB-70A came to a stop. The path,

when viewed from above, looked like an upside-down letter "J" because the aircraft had swung over half a mile to the right and had turned 110 degrees. Only the size of the lake bed made this landing possible; it is one major reason the Air Force tests at Edwards.

The damaged was quickly repaired and A/V-1 returned to flight on 22 March piloted by Cotton and Shepard on a 2 hour and 11 minute hop that only reached Mach 0.97 at 32,000 feet.

The only time an XB-70A would travel anywhere other than Edwards or Palmdale (not counting the last flight to the Air Force Museum) was on 24 March 1966 when Fulton and White took A/V-2 to the air show at Carswell AFB, Texas. The Valkyrie spent only 13 minutes at Mach 2.71 before slowing down, ending up at 6,000 feet over Carswell just 59 minutes after takeoff. For the next half

A/V-2 was one of the stars of the Carswell AFB airshow in March 1966. Note the simple sign that described the world's largest Mach 3 aircraft. (left: Terry Panopalis Collection; below: Fitz Fulton Collection)

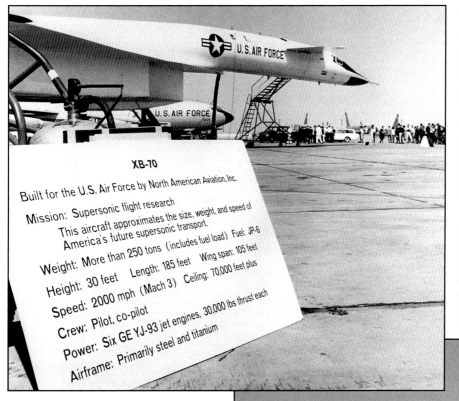

XB-70

Built for the U.S. Air Force by North American Aviation, Inc.

Mission: Supersonic flight research
This aircraft approximates the size, weight, and speed of America's future supersonic transport.

Weight: More than 250 tons (includes fuel load) Fuel: JP-6
Height: 30 feet   Length: 185 feet   Wing span: 105 feet
Speed: 2000 mph (Mach 3)   Ceiling: 70,000 feet plus
Crew: Pilot, co-pilot
Power: Six GE YJ-93 jet engines, 30,000 lbs thrust each
Airframe: Primarily steel and titanium

level itself out, the weight of the XB-70A forcing the gear into its normal position. As for the right gear … being behind the centerline of the main strut, it was unlikely that the gear would level out, but hopefully the landing would at least cause the gear to finish swinging into the direction of travel, and the wingtip would still clear the ground, although the right side would be much lower than the left.

hour, A/V-2 thundered around the skies of Texas before landing. The return flight two days later was the only flight during the entire program where performance data was not recorded, as Cotton and White flew back at subsonic speeds, taking a little over three hours to return to Edwards.

It was not unusual for the XB-70A to experience engine unstarts during the test program. For instance, on 12 April 1966 A/V-2 was on a high-speed flight that had been scheduled to fly at Mach 3 for 30 minutes, but Al White and Joe Cotton decided to cut the high-speed run short after an inlet unstart. The internal shock wave moved forward from its optimum position while the flight crew was experimenting with the manual vernier controls for "fine tuning" the engine inlets to achieve maximum performance. The unstart was aggravated by a turn maneuver – turning

always affected inlet airflow, but was usually compensated for by the automatic inlet control system.[6]

During the 20-minutes spent at Mach 3.08 and 72,800 feet, the maximum free-stream temperature reached 624 degF at stagnation points on the wing and inlet leading edges. The highest previous free-stream temperature had been 610 degF during a 16-minute Mach 3 flight on 8 April. The higher temperature on this flight was attributed to atmospheric conditions and not the duration of the flight.[7]

Not to outdone by her older sister, on 30 April 1966 the 37th flight of A/V-2 also experienced a landing gear problem. Shortly after takeoff, Cotton retracted the landing gear. However, a short-circuit in the landing gear retraction system permitted wind forces to blow the nose gear back into the partially-retracted gear

well door, slashing the tires. An attempt to lower the gear using the normal hydraulic system failed. Trying the backup electrical system, Cotton heard a "pop" as that system went dead.

White first brought the XB-70A around for a touch-and-go, hoping that a hard impact on the main gear would knock the nose gear loose and let it fall to the extended position. Even after a second try, however, the nose gear remained jammed. At this point, bailing out and losing the aircraft was quickly becoming the only option.

But there was fuel to burn, so White and Cotton circled around Edwards while engineers on the ground sorted things out. After more than 2 hours the problem with the backup system was traced – hopefully – to a circuit breaker. Now all Cotton had to do was find a way to short circuit

A/V-1 surrounded by ground equipment prior to an early morning flight at Edwards. Note the access ladder to the cockpit. (Chris Wamsley/Rockwell via the Terry Panopalis Collection)

The 37th flight of A/V-2 also had some excitement with the landing gear. It started with the nose gear impacting the gear door (above), resulting in multiple failures that made it impossible to lower the nose gear. Eventually, Joe Cotton shorted a circuit breaker with a paperclip. Unfortunately, three of the four main gear brakes remained engaged as the aircraft touched down, resulting in a fire during rollout. Damage was minimal. (Tony Landis Collection)

The first XB-70A flies formation with the NB-52B (008) on 6 January 1966. The two aircraft were roughly the same size, but the Valkyrie was about ten percent heavier. (U.S. Air Force via the Terry Panopalis Collection)

the unit. Of course, the Valkyrie had no onboard toolkit – that would have made things too simple. But Cotton had brought along his briefcase with his various notes and plans, and opening it, he found a binder-type paperclip. Straightening out the paperclip, then grasping the middle of it with a leather glove, Cotton

carefully reached in and short circuited the breaker. It did the trick.

However, the malfunction also caused hydraulic pressure to remain on three of the four main wheel brakes, which were thus locked when the aircraft landed at 173 knots. Fire fighters at Edwards pre-

vented any serious damage to the aircraft, which flew again a little over two weeks later.[8]

On 19 May during flight number 39, A/V-2 flew at Mach 3.06 at 72,500 feet for 33 minutes. In just 91 minutes, the Valkyrie traveled over 2,400 miles – an average speed of more than 1,500 miles per hour, including takeoff and landing. Finally, all remaining concerns about skin separation were laid to rest. The Valkyrie could lay claim to being a true Mach 3 cruiser.

Three days later A/V-2 thrilled the spectators at the Armed Forces Day show at Edwards, including a couple of supersonic passes over the crowd. Test data on stability and control issues were recorded during the 2-hour and 22-minute flight that reached Mach 1.51 and 36,500 feet.

With all systems tested, the XB-70A prepared to move into Part 2 of

A/V-2 shows three good drag chutes on the main runway at Edwards. The XB-70A program had a remarkable amount of trouble with drag chutes, although none caused any damage to the aircraft. (Gerald H. Balzer Collection)

The second aircraft banks over the flight line at Edwards. Note the black smoke from the six-pack of J93s. Despite her size, the XB-70A handled remarkably well during low-speed flight. (Rockwell via the Jay Miller Collection)

Phase Two test program, where NASA would become much more involved, and extensive sonic boom and handling tests would begin. New pilots would join the program, including NASA chief test pilot Joseph A. Walker, who had just come from the X-15 program. Not only did Walker have an "astronaut" rating (given to Air Force pilots who flew higher than 50 miles), he had flown the X-15 beyond Mach 6 (4,100 mph) in level flight. Mach 3 would seem slow. Also joining the program was Air Force Major Carl Cross. At the same time, both Al White and Joe Cotton began to gradually ease out of the program, with Cotton going on to test other aircraft for the Air Force, and White to work on other projects at North American.

A/V-2 was refitted with additional instrumentation and data recording equipment – more than a thousand sensors, recording devices) and telemetry equipment were installed. These instruments would give a better look at a number of phenomena that couldn't be thoroughly tested in a wind tunnel including body flex, flutter, and pressure distributions. At the same time, NASA began setting up a large number of ground sensors to precisely measure the effect of sonic booms. But tragedy awaited.

A/V-1 on 17 August 1965. Note that the intake and splitter area is not painted white as it was on A/V-2. (NASA DFRC Collection)

On 8 June 1966 Al White was the pilot of A/V-2 along with Carl Cross on his first flight as copilot. The flight was to consist of 12 subsonic airspeed calibration runs and a single sonic boom measurement run. Afterwards White and Cross were to rendezvous with a formation of other aircraft powered by General Electric engines for a public relations photographic session. General Electric had obtained local Air Force approval a week earlier for the photo session on a non-interference basis.

Participating in the photo session were a Northrop F-5A Freedom Fighter flown by GE test pilot John M. Fritz, who had organized the event; a Northrop T-38 Talon piloted by Captain Peter C. Hoag, with Joe Cotton in the rear seat; a McDonnell F-4B Phantom II flown by Navy Commander Jerome P. Skyrud with E.J. Black in the back; and a NASA F-104N (N813NA) flown by Joseph A. Walker. A Gates LearJet (also GE-powered) flown by H. Clay Lacey, loaded with photographers, recorded the event.

The rendezvous began at 08:27 on a southwesterly heading away from Edwards at 20,000 feet. By 08:43 all of the aircraft had formed up in a V-formation. The Valkyrie was leading – Walker's F-104N was off the starboard wing; Fritz's F-5 was outboard and to the rear of Walker; Skyrud's F-4 was off the port wing; Hoag's T-38 was outboard and to the rear of Skyrud. The LearJet was positioned about 200-yards to the left of the formation. For a good backdrop, White raised A/V-2 to 25,000 feet where he found blue sky. As the photo shoot progressed, the photographers asked several times for the formation to close up, until all five

The ill-fated formation just before the incident. Joe Walker's F-104N is under A/V-2's wing tip in the lower right corner. (AFFTC History Office Collection)

aircraft were in close proximity. At 09:26 the photographers were done, and everyone prepared to break formation and return to Edwards.

Suddenly, somebody shouted "mid-air ... mid-air ... mid-air" over the radio. The F-104N's tee-tail had hit the Valkyrie's drooped right wingtip and rolled sharply left, out of control.

The Starfighter then flipped upside down and passed over the Valkyrie inverted, shearing off part of its right and most of its left vertical stabilizer. Joe Walker was already dead.

Al White and Carl Cross heard the impact, but felt nothing. Flying in the T-38 off the left wingtip, Joe Cotton called out "207 [identifying

Seconds after the impact; Joe Walker is already dead. The XB-70A would continue to fly straight and level for 16 seconds. (AFFTC History Office Collection)

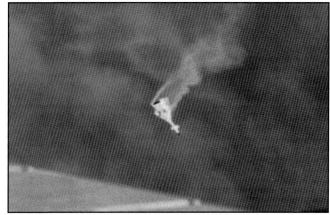

A/V-2 snap rolled to the right, then entered a flat spin. Al White managed to eject, but Carl Cross could not and perished in the accident. (AFFTC History Office Collection)

A/V-2] you've been hit! You've been hit!" But in those first moments, neither White nor Cross heard the call. Even as Cotton continued "okay, you're doing fine, he got the verticals, but you're still doing fine … Your tails are gone; You'll probably spin" neither B-70 pilot heard the "s" on tails and therefore didn't associate the mid-air collision with the XB-70A. White turned to Cross and asked "I wonder who got hit?" It would soon become obvious.

As if nothing had happened, the XB-70A flew straight and level for some 16 seconds. Then A/V-2 started a slight roll. Al White corrected the roll – and instantly recognized the peril as the XB-70A snap-rolled to the right. White tried to save A/V-2 – but after two slow rolls, the aircraft entered a flat spin, taking any hopes of recovery with it. White pushed his seat back to the eject position, but caught his arm in the capsule's clamshell doors as they closed. With the realization that he needed to get out quickly, White worked his arm clear and ejected just moments before A/V-2 impacted the ground a few miles north of Barstow, California.

Although the drogue chutes deployed from White's capsule, the airbag underneath the capsule – designed to absorb much of the impact – failed to inflate. Striking the ground, White took a 43-g impact – lessened to 33-g as his seat broke free of its mountings. Amazingly, although banged, battered, and bruised, he suffered no broken bones. White returned to flight status just three months later, but he never flew the XB-70A again.

Carl Cross was not so lucky. Still in his seat, he impacted the ground with A/V-2 and was killed. Cross was an 8,500-hour veteran of Korea and Vietnam, and had six years of testing in multi-engined jet aircraft.

The Valkyrie impacted the desert a few miles north of Barstow, California. The wing section (right) was a recongizable piece of the wreckage. (AFFTC History Office Collection)

Joe Walker had over 5,000 flight hours to his credit, including logging the highest flight of the X-15 program, as well as several Mach 6 flights. He had flown chase in NASA F-104s eight times before. Ironically, he was to become NASA's chief B-70 test pilot – his indoctrination flight was scheduled two days later in A/V-2.

The final cause of the mid-air was determined to be the inability of Joe Walker in the F-104N to discern that he had gradually closed-in on the XB-70A. The investigation board concluded that "… it is readily apparent that the movement of the F-104 from a position of safe clearance to one of contact was possible through gradual motion without the pilot's awareness. … The likelihood is further increased by the fact that at the position of impact of the F-104 horizontal stabilizer with the XB-70A drooped wing tip, the pilot's head was at least 10 ft. below the centerline of the [XB-70] fuselage."[9]

In their findings, the board concluded that air turbulence was not a contributing factor to the collision, based on telemetry that indicated no abrupt motions in pitch, roll, yaw, or acceleration. The board also ruled out the theory that airflow effects from the XB-70A somehow sucked the fighter into the bomber. The finding was that vortices contributed to the collision only after the F-104 was so close that collision was imminent. The board determined that there were no equipment problems with the XB-70A, and that there were no indications of malfunction on the F-104N, although the aircraft did not carry telemetry transmitters or recorders so there was no way to know for sure. Physiological problems were considered remote in any of the three pilots involved. Pilot distraction was considered unlikely, although a B-58 on a sonic boom run was approaching the formation during the last 16 seconds before the crash. The board did find that Joe Walker had no recent experience in flying the "loose V" formation, but discounted this as a real issue given Walker's extensive flight experience in general.[10]

The likely cause for Carl Cross' failure to eject, according to the board, was that the XB-70A went into a flat spin resulting in heavy forward forces. In order to eject, the seat must first be moved to its rearward position. White was believed to have initiated ejection slightly earlier during a period of lower g-forces. White confirmed that Cross had armed his capsule prior to takeoff.[11]

Serious issues were raised in Congress and the Department of Defense due to the fact that the mid-air collision had occurred while photographs were being taken for a private company. Two boards were appointed to investigate the crash. A memorandum from Secretary of the Air Force Harold Brown to Secretary

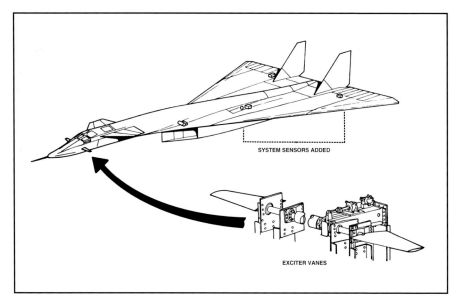

SYSTEM SENSORS ADDED

EXCITER VANES

Following A/V-1's 73rd flight NASA installed a structural dynamics research package called ILAF (identically located acceleration and force). Two exciter vanes – each about two feet long – were located just in front of the crew compartment. They could rotate 12 degrees at a frequency up to 8 cycles per second. The vanes induced structural vibrations having a known frequency and amplitude; accelerometers sensed the disturbances and signaled the aircraft's stability augmentation system to move the aircraft's controls and suppress the disturbance. NASA hoped the ILAF program would serve as a prototype for advanced systems that could be installed on SSTs, enabling them to fly with increased smoothness and reducing the fatigue experienced by both passengers and airframe. Previously, XB-70A crews had frequently experienced annoying trim changes and buffeting from clear air turbulence and rapidly fluctuating atmospheric temperature. Test results indicated that the ILAF system reduced the buffeting associated with such conditions. The XB-70A made its first ILAF-equipped flight on 11 June 1968; from then until the end of the program in 1969, the aircraft acquired a great deal of information applicable to the design of future SST or large supersonic military aircraft. A similar system was installed on the North American/Boeing B-1 bomber. (NASA)

of Defense Robert S. McNamara contained the findings. Blame was placed on three Air Force colonels – Colonel Albert M. Cate (deputy for systems test at Edwards), Colonel Joseph F. Cotton (XB-70A test director), and Colonel James G. Smith, the public information officer who had failed to notify Air Force Systems Command of the photography session. All three colonels were reprimanded. A Systems Command civilian, John S. McCollum, who was at Edwards the day prior to the tragedy and had been briefed on the photo-taking session on 7 June, was also reprimanded for not using his authority to stop the flight. [12]

NASA TAKES OVER

Prior to the loss of A/V-2, the aircraft had become a surrogate for the proposed Boeing 733 SST. The government and private researchers embarked on a major sonic boom test program at Edwards in an effort to accurately forecast psychological reaction and structural damage associated with overpressures from supersonic transports. The National Sonic Boom Program (NSBP) was set up by the President's Office of Science and Technology, and consisted of three principal participants – the Air Force, NASA, and Stanford Research Institute.

NASA also installed rake probes on top of the fuselage and wing. The outline area was done in red and masks a "No Step" zone for the tubing running across the upper surface of the wing going to the probe. These photos were taken on 17 March 1967. (NASA DFRC Collection)

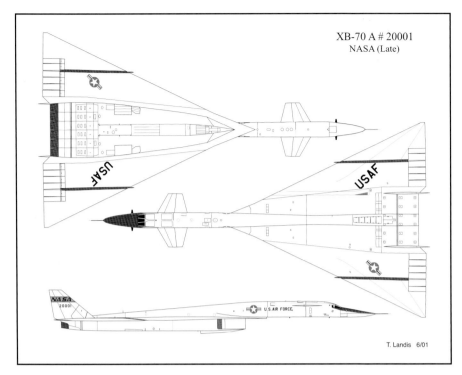

XB-70 A # 20001
NASA (Late)

T. Landis 6/01

When A/V-1 was turned over to NASA she received the traditional yellow tail stripe, and the area around the intakes was repainted white. Various photo reference markings were applied periodically, and some experiments also altered the exterior slightly such as the exciter vanes shown here. (Drawn by Tony Landis)

No matter the angle, the XB-70A looks futuristic even 30 years after its last flight. So far there has been little use for the experience gained from flying a large Mach 3 aircraft, and there is no direct application on the horizon even now. Still, it was a remarkable achievement. (AFFTC History Office Collection)

A sonic boom is caused by the overpressure created by a shock wave produced by a supersonic aircraft. The overpressure could be potentially disturbing and destructive to persons and objects on the ground. The XB-70A was selected to perform the tests because it most closely approximated the size of the Boeing SST. It was felt that the Valkyrie was the only aircraft capable of simulating the SST primarily because weight and size had a marked affect on sonic boom signatures. Although overpressures of equal peak magnitudes could be obtained with F-104s and B-58s, the duration of the boom itself varied with each aircraft as do the shape of the shock waves themselves and the forces involved.

The NSBP began on 6 June 1966 when A/V-2 performed the initial sonic boom test, reaching Mach 3.05 at 72,000 feet. The second NSBP test was on 8 June – however, it was followed by the mid-air collision that destroyed A/V-2.

Both the Air Force and NASA were unsure that A/V-1, with her Mach 2.5 speed limitation, could continue the research since the Boeing SST was envisioned as a Mach 2.7 aircraft. A/V-1 had not flown since 9 May because the original test program was scheduled to end in early June. Nevertheless, given that A/V-1 was the only large supersonic aircraft available, NASA decided to install a duplicate set of test equipment in A/V-1. During this period A/V-1 was also equipped with improved escape capsules and an automated AICS, thereby eliminating its troublesome manual air induction control system.

A/V-1 took to the air again on 3 November 1966 with Cotton and Fulton at the controls. Some 250

sonic boom tests were planned, mostly at overpressures of 1.5 to 3.0 pounds per square foot, but some would reach 4.0 psf. The proposed 300,000 pound SST, cruising at Mach 2.7 at 65,000 feet, was expected to generate an overpressure of 2.0 psf.

The ninth and final flight of the NSBP was on 17 January 1967. Scientists saw little point in continuing the program since the XB-70A flights had already provided sufficient data about large aircraft overpressures. It was found that sonic booms were affected by many factors – temperature inversions, Mach number at altitude fluctuations, unparalleled shock waves, and variations in aircraft weight , size, and shape.[13]

Because both the Air Force and NASA had equally allocated funds for the NSBP, it remained a joint Air Force/NASA venture – directed by NASA, managed by the Air Force. At the conclusion of the NSBP, the Air Force announced it was leaving the XB-70A program because of budget problems. In early 1967 NASA formally took over the XB-70A flight research program. The Air Force's withdrawal forced flight rates from the expected two flights per month to a single flight.

Flights for the last 18 months concentrated on basic research, although much of it was applicable to the SST program. Between January and April 1967, additional instrumentation designed to measure structural response to gusts, stability and control, boundary layer noise, and SST simulation was installed. These included wing rakes on the right wing for measuring the boundary layer, microphones in the lower nose section for measuring boundary layer noise, instruments to measure gusts and dynamic response of the air-

A view from the bottom of A/V-1 during her tenure at NASA. Although beautiful when clean, the white paint showed dirt easily – most of what is on the lower fuselage is tire and runway dust from landings. (Mike Machat Collection)

frame, and additional performance instrumentation. The first NASA flight occurred on 25 April 1967 with Joe Cotton and Fitz Fulton at the controls. Twenty-three additional flights were completed, and the highest speed attained during this phase was Mach 2.55 at 67,000 feet.[14]

RETIREMENT

By the end of 1968, increasing operating expenses and maintenance problems had caught up with A/V-1. The research data gained from the aircraft no longer justified the resources needed to maintain and operate it. On 13 January 1969, NASA Headquarters announced termination of the XB-70A flight research program. The announcement rightly hailed the XB-70A as "a productive flight research vehicle for studying sonic boom, flight dynamics, and handling problems associated with the development of

Two of the fastest aircraft ever built – both by North American Aviation – pose together at Edwards in 1967. The first XB-70A could fly at 2,000 mph (Mach 3); the X-15A-2 (56-6671) would eventually record 4,520 mph (Mach 6.7). (NASA)

At altitude with the wing tips in the mid-down position. The rake experiment may be seen, and several photo-reference marks have been painted on the fuselage. Note the open afterburner exhaust nozzles. (Mike Machat Collection)

advanced supersonic aircraft." The final NASA flight was originally scheduled for 22 January 1969, but was delayed until 4 February when A/V-1 took off for Wright-Patterson AFB, outside Dayton, Ohio.

Fitz Fulton and Ted Sturmthal were the pilots on the flight to the Air Force Museum. A trooper to the end, the XB-70A continued to record research data even during this 3 hour and 17 minute trip. The 1,880 mile flight was made at Mach 0.92 and 29,000 feet. Fitz Fulton made a single pass over the runway before bringing the XB-70A down for a perfect landing – ironically marking the first time that A/V-1 had gotten three 100-percent drag chutes. This was the 83rd flight of A/V-1 and its log book was closed showing a total flight time of 160 hours, 16 minutes.

Fitz Fulton turned the aircraft log book over to the curator of the Air Force Museum. The total cost of the B-70 program has been reported as $1,500 million, so it cost about $11.6 million per flight – including both aircraft and a total of 129 flight tests between them. This rather staggering statistic is what reportedly prompted Ted Sturmthal to say, "I'd do anything to keep the B-70 in the air – except pay for it myself."[15]

The first XB-70A lands at Wright-Patterson AFB on its delivery flight to the Air Force Museum. With this flight, the largest Mach 3 aircraft in the world passed into the history books. (Jim Tuttle Collection)

[1] "XB-70A 's Research Role will Contribute Mach 3 Flight Data for SST Development," *Aviation Week & Space Technology*, 18 May 1964, pp. 26-27. [2] The majority of this chapter is derived from the XB-70 Flight Log compiled by Betty Love, DFRC, dated 7 May 1969, and various pilot and flight reports in the files of the DFRC History Office. Other published reports are cited where appropriate. [3] Marcelle Size Knaack, *Post-World War II Bombers*, (Washington DC: Office of Air Force History, 1988), pp. 572-573; "XB-70 Flight," *Aviation Week & Space Technology*, 28 September 1964, pp. 25-26. [4] *Post-World War II Bombers*, pp. 572-573; "XB-70 Flight," *Aviation Week & Space Technology*, 28 September 1964, pp. 25-26; XB-70 Flight Log compiled by Betty Love, DFRC, dated 7 May 1969. [5] "XB-70 Flight," *Aviation Week & Space Technology*, 28 September 1964, pp. 25-26. [6] "XB-70A Inlet Unstart," *Aviation Week & Space Technology*, 25 April 1966, p. 99; XB-70 Flight Log compiled by Betty Love, DFRC, dated 7 May 1969. [7] Ibid. [8] "Inflight Repairs Overcome XB-70 Malfunction," *Aviation Week & Space Technology*, 8 May 1966; XB-70 Flight Log compiled by Betty Love, DFRC, dated 7 May 1969. [9] "XB-70 Crash Findings Reported By Air Force Investigating Board," *Aviation Week & Space Technology*, 22 August 1966, p. 18. [10] Ibid. [11] Ibid. [12] Ibid. [13] "NASA Assumes XB-70 Research Effort," *Aviation Week & Space Technology*, 13 February 1967, p. 38. [14] Ibid. [15] Air Force Press Release, 5 February 1969.

THE RIDE TO VALHALLA

The XB-70A was truly one of the aerospace wonders of the 1960s – at the time of her first flight, she was the heaviest aircraft ever built, and also the fastest.

To the eye, the two prototypes differed in only minor details – a keen observer would notice the change in dihedral on the wing; most noticed the black radome under the nose. As was the norm for prototypes of the era, neither aircraft carried any special markings or names; only the standard U.S. AIR FORCE and stars-and-bars.

Later in her life, AV/1 had the typical NASA yellow band painted on the outside of each vertical stabilizer, but was otherwise largely not changed by her new masters.

Interestingly, production aircraft would likely not have been white. Most of the available documentation indicates that the special infrared coatings being developed for the B-70s would have been a strange opaque silver color. The stillborn F-108 would probably have been similarly finished. Whether the coatings would have worked is an open question.

The XF-108 mockup sometime before the mockup inspection in January 1958. By the time of the inspection, the mockup had been painted white and moved to the same area that would later house the B-70 mockup. The mockup was constructed of metal. (Boeing Historical Archives)

By this time the mockup generally resembled the aircraft that would be built, although the shape of the upper aft fuselage is not nearly as blended as it would be on the actual aircraft. Note the location of the U.S. AIR FORCE marking on the lower fuselage and the SAC band behind the canard. (Chris Wamsley/Rockwell via the Terry Panopalis Collection)

A partially-completed A/V-1 sees the light of day for a while. At this point the major fuselage assembly is complete but the wings still need to be added. Note the fixed portions of the vertical stabilizers at the rear of the fuselage. (Chris Wamsley/Rockwell via the Terry Panopalis Collection)

A/V-1 a short time later shows the vertical stabilizers have been attached. The stainless steel honeycomb sandwich that made up the majority of the skin was a dark gunmetal color. Note the details inside the wing joint. (Chris Wamsley/Rockwell via the Terry Panopalis Collection)

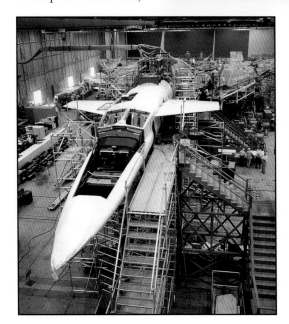

A/V-1 before and after the movable windshield ramp has been installed. In the background, the wings are being joined with the fuselage, a painstaking welding job due to the honeycomb construction technique. (Boeing Historical Archives)

A/V-2 gives a good comparison to the only other supersonic U.S. Air Force bomber, the Convair B-58 Hustler. A B-58 was frequently used as a chase plane since it had much longer legs than the T-38s normally used. Regardless, it still could not keep up with the B-70 in either speed or range.
(Jay Miller Collection)

The small flap on the canard helped minimize the rotation angle, but like all delta-wing aircraft, the Valkyrie still took-off and landed nose high. Note how close to the ground the afterburner exhausts are during rotation. It would have been interesting to watch how close the proposed "alert pod" would have come to scraping.
(Gerald H. Balzer Collection)

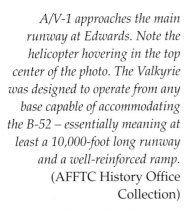

A/V-1 approaches the main runway at Edwards. Note the helicopter hovering in the top center of the photo. The Valkyrie was designed to operate from any base capable of accommodating the B-52 – essentially meaning at least a 10,000-foot long runway and a well-reinforced ramp.
(AFFTC History Office Collection)

A/V-2 makes a low pass down the flight line at Edwards with her wingtips in the mid-down position. Despite her size, the Valkyrie handled decently. (AFFTC History Office Collection)

A/V-1 being prepared for her first flight on the ramp at Palmdale. Note the access ladders to the cockpit and the air intakes. (Tony Landis Collection)

During December 1967, NASA used A/V-1 for a series of engine runs to measure noise in support of the SST program. Note the microphones set up on tall poles in the background. Also noteworthy is the amount of black smoke from the J93 engines. (Chris Wamsley/Rockwell via the Terry Panopalis Collection)

A/V-1 taxies past the Edwards tower on her first NASA Flight – 25 April 1967. The changes in markings were limited to the traditional yellow NASA tail stripe, and small NASA "meatballs" under the cockpit windows. (NASA DFRC Collection)

WARBIRDTECH
SERIES

Operating and maintaining an aircraft as complex as the XB-70A was not easy. Note all of the ground support equipment surround the aircraft during an engine run-up. (AFFTC History Office Collection)

A/V-1 roll-out on 11 May 1964. It must have been interesting for the tug driver – who is used to being in front of the airplane he is towing – since a large part of the Valkyrie's neck was in front of the tug. (Tony Landis Collection)

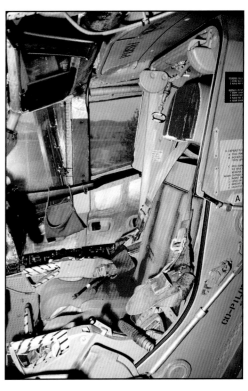

The copilot escape capsule in A/V-1. The capsule was a great idea, despite its demonstrated 50-percent success rate. (Terry Panopalis)

One of the 38 YJ93-GE-3 engines built to support the XB-70A program. This was an advanced engine for the day, pioneering air-cooled turbine blades and titanium construction. The engine was optimized to run in continuous afterburner at Mach 3. The connection for the drive shaft that ran the airframe-mounted accessories package can be seen under the front of the engine. The package under the engine also contained the engine hydraulic system and its control system. (G.E. Aircraft Engines via the Terry Panopalis Collection)

A YJ93 engine being installed in the No. 4 position of A/V-1. The afterburner nozzle is closed in this photo. Note that the vertical stabilizers have not been installed on the aircraft – this was likely a test-fit of the engine, not the final installation. (Chris Wamsley/Rockwell via the Terry Panopalis Collection)

A good close-up of the lower aft fuselage. Note the numbers on each engine bay. The elevons were particularly long and narrow, but provided decent control authority at both high and low speeds. The wings are at the mid-down position here, meaning that the outer two elevons were locked in their neutral position. Also noteworthy is the angle of the national insignia on the underside of the wing – the one on top was similarly angled. (NASA Collection)

In her element, A/V-1 folds her wing tips to the full-down position and prepares to go fast. There are no photos of the Valkyries at high Mach numbers simply because no aircraft could keep up with them past Mach 2, and few could fly as high. A/V1 only flew to Mach 3 once before being restricted to Mach 2.5 because of material problems with her honeycomb skin. (Tony Landis Collection)

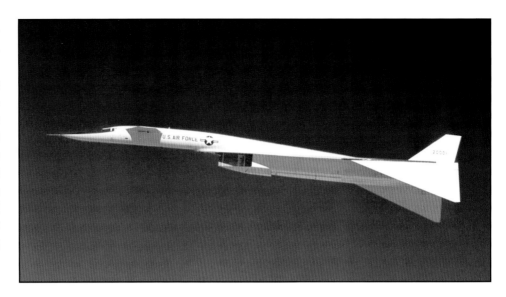

A/V-1 on her first flight on 21 September 1964. Note that the engine area was not painted at this point — it would receive its coat of white paint when the aircraft was repainted following the structural tests before flight No. 5. (AFFTC History Office Collection)

The two fastest air-breathing aircraft in the world pose together during a display at Edwards AFB on 1 May 1965. A/V-1 shows the great size different between the XB-70A and one of the Lockheed YF-12As (06935). The Valkyrie was almost five times as heavy as the blackbird, but had essentially the same performance. (AFFTC History Office Collection)

A/V-2 was the subject of a wonderful set of photographs taken at low-level around the desert and mountains of the southwest United States. It was a different photo shoot that would ultimately lead to her demise. (Rockwell via the Jay Miller Collection)

A sight that was somewhat elusive – three fully-opened drag chutes. Note the deployed flap on the trailing edge of the canard and the drag chute compartment door on top of the fuselage. The landing gear doors were closed except when the gear was in motion. (Rockwell via the Jay Miller Collection)

Five XB-70 principles at the 30th anniversary celebration held at Edwards in September 1994. From the left: Joe Cotton, Al White, Walt Spivak, Fitz Fulton, and Don Mallick. Walt Spivak was the chief designer; the other four were pilots (Tony Landis)

THE D4ETAILS

As built, the two XB-70As were two-seat high-performance demonstrators, not truly prototype bombardment aircraft. For the most part, the following description applies to the as-built configuration; the differences between the two air vehicles are noted as appropriate. Where they are known, the details of any possible production bomber are also included.

For the record, the third air vehicle had not progressed into final assembly before it was cancelled. However, a great deal of the material had been produced: all of the 24,452 square feet of honeycomb core had been received, as had all of the 157,846 pounds of other sheet metal (not all of it would have been used – some would have been lost during machining, etc.). Over ninety percent of the extrusions and forgings had been produced. Most of the "neck" had been roughed-in, with the bottom deck finished, the top deck 90 percent complete, and all other sections at least 50 percent complete. The landing gear had been received by North American. No exact record of the fate of the material could be found, although it is assumed that it was scrapped at the end of the program.

The XB-70A had truly remarkable performance – the maximum design speed exceeded Mach 3 at altitudes up to 85,000 feet. The maximum taxi weight was 542,029 pounds and the maximum takeoff weight was 532,640 pounds. Maximum landing weight was 524,209 pounds. However, after a main landing gear bogie was repaired on A/V-1, the maximum allowable weight was reduced to 520,000 pounds.[1]

FORWARD FUSELAGE

The XB-70A was characterized by a long forward fuselage "neck," with a canard located just aft of the flight deck. At touchdown, the pilot was 30 feet above the ground and 110 feet ahead of the main landing gear. Given that the delta-wing XB-70A touched down decidedly nose-up (as do all deltas), instead of the level profile used by the B-52, it would have required some major adjustments by operational pilots.

The fuselage was a semi-monocoque structure of basically circular section, changing to a flat-top section in the crew compartment area. The forward fuselage was made of riveted titanium frames and skin over longerons of H-11 steel (often called "tool steel"). The large nose radome that would have housed the attack and navigation radars was manufactured from laminated Vibran.[2]

COCKPIT

The pilot and copilot sat side-by-side in individual escape capsules. AV/3 and operational aircraft would have had offensive and defensive systems operators sitting behind the two pilots. Each escape capsule had a self-contained oxygen and pressurization system, affording complete crew protection during and following ejection. The capsules could also be closed, if necessary, for crew protection during an in-flight emergency, particularly one that involved the decompression of the crew compartment. Limited control of the aircraft and engines (throttle down only) was possible from inside the closed capsules, which had a window on the front edge that allowed the pilot to see the instrument panel. When the capsules were closed the

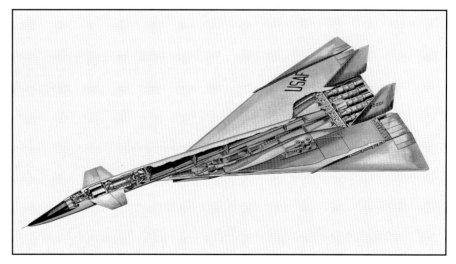

General cutaway view of the XB-70A. Despite her large size, every cubic inch was used to house fuel, systems, or the massive air intakes. (Tony Landis Collection)

A nice view of the flight deck of A/V-1 without the escape capsules installed. The large fuel control panel is on the left side of the copilot's control wheel. Instrumentation was a mix of conventional round dials and vertical tapes. Getting into and out of the escape capsules was awkward, at best, and the width of the center console did not make it any easier. To partially solve the problem, North American hinged the center console (right). (Jim Tuttle Collection)

crew microphones went "hot" to provide continuous communication. The capsules provided meaningful escape from zero to 80,000 feet and 100 to 2,000 mph.[3]

The encapsulation and ejection cycles were controlled by handgrips within the capsules. Raising the handgrips automatically encapsulated the crewman, while squeezing a trigger within the handgrip jettisoned the escape hatch and ejected the capsule. A rocket catapult propelled the capsule from the aircraft and clear of the vertical stabilizers, while stabilization booms deployed to prevent the capsule from tumbling. As the capsule descended, barometrically-controlled actuators deployed the recovery parachute and impact attenuator. The extended stabilization booms provided the capsule with a self-righting characteristic in the event of water landing, and the capsule was water tight and could float for prolonged periods if necessary. An Air Force volunteer actually survived 72 hours afloat in a B-70 capsule in January 1960. Survival equipment was provided in four separate kits in each capsule, mounted on the upper left and right walls, and under the capsule floor.

The equipment consisted of cold weather clothing, a life raft, sustenance gear, signaling equipment, first aid kit, and rations. [4]

The B-70 instrument panels were a mixture of traditional round instruments and the unique vertical "tape" instruments that found brief favor during the 1960s. The instruments were color-coded and illuminated by white light (the traditional red light washes out color).

In theory the XB-70As provided a "shirt sleeve" environment, but in fact every flight over 50,000 feet was conducted with the crew in pressure suits. The crew compartment temperature could be regulated between 42 degF and 105 degF, according to crew preferences. A constant pressure altitude of 8,000 feet was maintained under normal circumstances, and an emergency ram air system could maintain a pressure altitude of 40,000 feet (requiring oxygen, but not pressure suits) in the event of a primary system failure. [v]

The main crew entrance was on the left side of the aircraft, forward of the canard. This entrance was 17 feet above ground level, requiring special access stands for ingress and egress. Care had to be taken to ensure the access stand did not touch the fuselage since rubbing could result in minor surface damage that would be aggravated by Mach 3 flight. There were four separate hatches in the upper fuselage, corresponding to the positions of the expected four-person crew in any future production version. In the XB-70As, the two forward hatches were ballistically removed in the event of crew ejection; the two aft hatches could be ballistically or manually removed for aircrew escape during ground emergencies. [vi]

The aircraft had two windshields – a moveable outer unit and a fixed inner unit. The moveable windshield and ramp assembly consisted of five full-tempered glass panels in a framework structure that was hinged at the forward end and guided by four frame-mounted roller assemblies. In the full-up position, the slope of the ramp and windshield formed a nose section contour that provided minimal drag. In the full-down position, a 24-degree slope provided increased visibility for low-speed operations. Intermediate positions could be selected as necessary. The moveable windshield

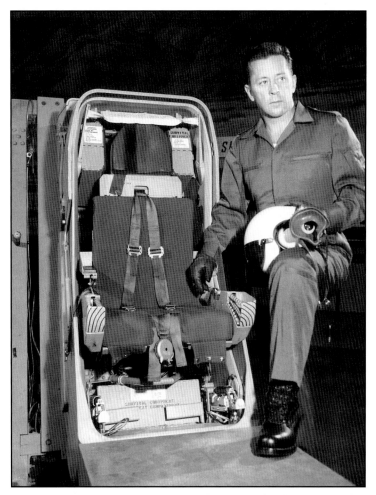

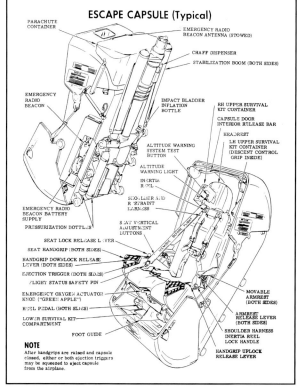

The escape capsule drawing from the XB-70A flight manual (above), and Al White stands by a capsule outside the aircraft (left). (above: U.S. Air Force; Left: Gerald H. Balzer Collection)

A great close-up of the canopy area during a test flight on 2 December 1965. The ramp is in the up (streamlined) position. (NASA DFRC Collection)

and ramp assembly was hydraulically operated and electrically controlled. An emergency system was provided that allowed the ramp to be fully lowered in the event the primary system failed. A windshield anti-ice and rain removal system directed high-temperature (600 degF) engine extraction air through two nozzles on the leading edge of the movable windshield. The inner fixed windshield consisted of five glass panels in a 78-inch wide, 200 pound 7Al-4Mo titanium forging. A defogging system was provided for the inner surface of both the movable and fixed windscreens.[7]

CANARDS

The canard served primarily as a trimming device. but could be used in conjunction with the elevons for additional pitch control under some circumstances. The entire canard could be deflected from zero to six degrees for trim control, and the trailing edge could be lowered 20 degrees to function as a flap. The leading edge sweep was 31.70 degrees with a total area of 265.28 square feet (415.59 square feet including the fuselage portion). The canard was constructed from a torsion box made of corrugated titanium spars and skin panels. The leading edges were made from stainless steel honeycomb sandwich, and the trailing edge flaps were titanium.[8]

WINGS

The wing had an aspect ratio of 1.751:1, with a mean chord of 117.75 feet at the root and 2.25 feet at the tip. The leading edge was swept back at 65.56 degrees and the total area was 6,297.15 square feet. The entire upper and lower wing surface was covered with brazed stainless steel honeycomb sandwich panels welded together. The leading edges were attached directly to the front spar. The spars were of the sine-wave webbed type. A/V-1 had no anhedral, but the second aircraft featured 5 degrees of dihedral. Both aircraft had a slight aerodynamic twist on the outer panel leading edge. The wing-to-fuselage joint was 80 feet long and both the inner and outer honeycomb face sheets of the upper and lower wing surfaces had to be welded together. The first step welded the inner edge of the honeycomb using a tungsten electrode inserted

through a 0.125-inch gap between the outer face sheets. The latter were then joined with a filler strip welded with an electron-beam gun to minimize shrinkage. In all, there were over 6 miles of welding during component assembly and 2.5 miles of welding during final assembly; several of these miles involved the edges of fuel tanks.[9]

The outer 40-percent (span-wise) of each wing could be folded downward to increase directional stability during high-speed flight. Each tip occupied about 500 square feet of area and was driven by six Curtiss-Wright 32,000:1 motor hinges housed under a black magnesium-thorium fairing. On production aircraft the leading edge of the fairing would have housed an infrared sensor for the defensive avionics. The wing tips could be commanded to three positions: UP, 1/2 (25 degrees down on A/V-1 and 30 degrees on A/V-2), and DOWN (64.5 degrees on A/V-1 and 69.5 degrees on A/V-2). The UP position was used or landing, take-off, and subsonic flight. The 1/2 position was used for supersonic flight, while the DOWN position was used at very high speeds (Mach 2.5 and up). The use of the folding wing tips eliminated the increased drag that would have resulted if larger vertical stabilizers had been used instead. When the tips were full down, the shock wave they generated impinged on the bottom surface of the wing, adding about 5 percent more lift to the compression lift already being generated.[10]

At first the design folded the outer 20 percent of each wing; i.e., outboard of the outer elevon. However, wind tunnel models soon indicated that additional surface area was required for directional stability, so the fold line was moved inboard to

between the fourth and fifth elevon. This led to some complications since as-built the outer two elevon sections were now located on the folding part of each wing tip. A wing fold disengage system was incorporated that automatically locked the outer two elevon sections on each wing at the neutral position and disengaged them from further movement until the wings were unfolded. Weight-on-wheels sensors prevented the wings from being folded on the ground since the tips would impact the ground in the full down position. An emergency up system was provided in the event the two primary systems failed to return the wings to the up position during flight.[11]

Elevons at the wing trailing edge were segmented into six sections per side to reduce air load bending effects. Two hydraulic actuators powered each elevon segment, which could move 30 degrees up or down from the centerline. Symmetrical movement of the elevons provided basic pitch control; differential movement provided roll control.[12]

The XB-70As used a flight augmentation control system that used electrical signals in parallel with the mechanical linkage between the control columns and hydraulically-actuated flight controls. The actual deflection of the flight control panels was primarily by the mechanical linkage; the electrical control provided a small degree (either the same as, or opposite of the mechanical) of deflection for trim purposes. The augmentation system also provided automatic damping about all three axes.[13]

VERTICAL STABILIZERS

The vertical stabilizers had a leading edge sweep of 51.76 degrees and 233.96 square feet of area. Interesting-ly, if North American had not opted for the folding wingtips, the vertical stabilizers would have needed 467.92 square feet to provide equivalent directional stability. Only the forward lower edge (about a third of the area) was fixed; the rest of the surface was used as a rudder driven by dual hydraulic actuators. The hinge line was located at 45 degrees from the vertical. The rudders could deflect 12 degrees either side of center.

The fixed supporting base was a multi-spar design with honeycomb skin panels. It was attached to the wing root juncture by mechanical fasteners. The movable rudders were also multi-spar with brazed honeycomb skin panels. The leading and trailing edges were full-depth honeycomb wedges.[14]

LOWER FUSELAGE

The aft fuselage was a hybrid structure consisting of a variety of different construction techniques. During high speed flight the external skin temperatures of certain areas could reach 675 degF, while the internal temperatures could exceed 900 degF in the aft fuselage due to engine heat. Since the engines occupied most of the last 26 feet of the lower fuselage and the air intakes and weapons bay occupied most of the forward section, North American could not use full-depth transverse framing. In order to carry the wing bending loads across the fuselage, North American used multiple shallow-depth crossbeams to form the upper part of the bent. The side and lower transverse frames supported the engine access doors and were used to complete the bent. The spars were machined from H-11 and used titanium webs. At the side of the fuselage, the honeycomb sandwich wing stub was joined to the H-11 frames with high-strength mechanical fasteners. The skin covering the top and sides of the lower fuselage was 6A104V titanium alloy riveted in place. The engine compartment doors used 6A1-4V titanium alloy skins over 4A1-3Mo-1V titanium frames.[15]

The original B-70 design included

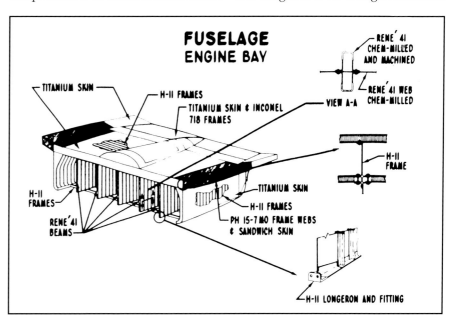

The engine bay was made up of a variety of exotic materials, including René 41, titanium, and H-11 tool steel. (North American Aviation)

The intakes on the XB-70A were huge – each trio of J93 engines required a vast amount of air at full power, and the intakes had to both supply the air and slow it down. The photo at left shows the middle of the right air intake looking forward. Note the person for scale. The photo at right was taken from about where the person was sitting, looking rearward toward the empty engine locations. (Tony Landis Collection)

two weapons bays. When it became obvious that the high energy fuel program would not materialize and the new bomber would have to rely on less-efficient JP6, the aft weapons bay was converted into additional fuel storage. As built, the 29-foot long weapons bay on the XB-70As extended from fuselage station YF1356* to YF1704. The opening of the bay was seven feet above ground level. The bay was covered by two sets of doors operating on a single set of tracks. The length of the track permitted only one set of doors to be opened at a time. Moving both doors aft opened the forward 14 feet of the bay; moving only the aft door opened the rear 14 feet of the bay. The center one foot was unusable since the doors never cleared the area. This also meant that weapons longer than about 13 feet could not be carried by the B-70. In the closed position the leading edge of the forward door was held tight against the step fairing of the fuselage by two interconnected hooks that engaged the fuselage structure. The aft door was locked to

the forward door in an identical manner. It should be noted that the weapons bay doors on A/V-1 and A/V-2 were not powered and could not be opened in flight. AV/3 would have had powered doors, as well as suspension and release equipment in the rear portion of the weapons bay for a single type of weapon for demonstration purposes.[16]

AIR INDUCTION

As with any supersonic aircraft, a way had to be found to reduce the engine intake air to subsonic velocities. In the XB-70A, two completely separate and independent inlet duct systems were provided, each delivering air to three engines. Each intake was about seven feet high at the splitter. From there the air was ducted approximately 80 feet back to a plenum chamber just ahead of the engines. The plenum chamber was the size of a small bedroom. The rectangular-section intake was manufactured from brazed stainless steel honeycomb sandwich panels except for H-11 steel sections around the

front of the engines. The primary function of the Hamilton Standard inlet control system was to position the shock waves created at supersonic speeds so that the air entering the engines was subsonic. Each duct system incorporated a rectangular variable-geometry inlet, a variable area bypass, a boundary layer bleed air control, and an air inlet control system (AICS). Varying the inlet geometry was accomplished by a movable panel system in each inlet duct. Each inlet had three fixed ramps, three movable panels, plenum divider panels that isolated four compartments just inboard of the inlet, and hydraulic actuators to position the panels. The ramps and panels served three primary functions: they formed the inlet duct wall, set up a shock wave pattern during supersonic flight, and provided a means of bleeding the boundary layer air.[17]

---

* The Cartesian coordinate system used on the XB-70 was generally the same as used by almost all aircraft. The coordinate system used X, Y, and Z to designate the axis; subscript F was used for the fuselage, W for the wing, etc. In the case of the Valkyrie, the zero coordinate of the fuselage was located 128 inches ahead of the nose; i.e., the nose (ignoring the pitot boom) was at YF128.

Approximately 90 percent of the air compression was performed in the inlet, not the engine. The inlet was designed to reduce the free-stream air velocity from Mach 3 to less than Mach 1 by a series of shocks, beginning with the primary shock wave created by the leading edge of the splitter duct and ending aft of the minimum throat area. Ideally, the terminal shock wave would have been at the minimum throat area. But factors such as gust disturbances could "pop" the shock outside the inlet, resulting in an "unstart" and possible engine flameout. Engineers decided to accept a small performance penalty and move the shock further aft in an attempt to prevent this from happening.[18]

Two secondary shocks prior to the duct entrance were caused by breaks in the sweep of the splitter duct. The air followed a circular route in the duct, which caused another series of shocks. The terminal shock to subsonic velocity was the last to occur. Three movable panels, positioned by two hydraulic actuators, opened or closed the throat area to meet engine air requirements; the maximum opening was 48 inches wide while the minimum was 19 inches. A three-position switch in the cockpit allowed the pilots to choose how far back the terminal shock would be positioned. For maximum range and most efficient air recovery, the shock was positioned forward. However, if the aircraft was flying through turbulent air or maneuvering, the shock would be positioned further back. The aft position provided the most stable operation and basically precluded the shock from being expelled through the front of the duct.[19]

Excess inlet air was jettisoned overboard through six pairs of bypass doors located on the upper surface of the wing between and slightly forward of the vertical stabilizers. The six sets of doors were divided into two sets of trimmer doors and four sets of primary doors. Each pair of doors was interconnected (one door opened downward and the other opened upward). The bypass doors provided from zero to 2,400 square inches of bypass area.[20]

The three panels in the throat of each inlet were perforated so that slow-moving turbulent boundary layer air was bled to ambient pressure on the other side of the panels into four separate plenums, each bleeding boundary air from a different section of the forward duct. This air was discharged at the rear of the step just aft of the nose wheel well. The remaining boundary layer air was diverted into the engine compartments to provide cooling. This air exited from ducts around the engines. North American believed that ducting inlet bleed air around the engines would also effectively cloak the afterburner from infrared detection. However, little could be done about the miles-long trail of hot gases generated by the six J93s.[21]

Two pairs of unstart sensors were in a support package located between the throat panel hydraulic actuating cylinder and the outboard wall of the forward weapons bay. An inlet unstart was "an undesirable condition resulting from the expulsion of the terminal normal shock wave during flight when it is desired to have it located inside the duct." The air induction control system package was located in the aft weapons bay, complete with its own environmental control system. This equipment would have been relocated in any production version.[22]

LANDING GEAR

Cleveland Pneumatic manufactured tricycle landing gear that had dual steerable nose wheels and four wheels on each main gear bogie. The

The nose gear used the same size wheels and tires as the main gear. This is A/V-2 on 25 March 1966. (NASA DFRC Collection)

The main gear retraction sequence was complicated in order that the gear could fit into relatively small gear wells that did not interfere with the air intakes. This sequence of photos was taken on 4 May 1967. (NASA DFRC Collection)

gear retracted into environmentally-controlled compartments in the lower fuselage. The nose gear retraction was aft; the main gear went through a complicated folding and rotation sequence to fit into relatively small compartments while not interfering with the air intakes or engine plenum chambers. The wheel well doors were kept closed except when the gear was being extended or retracted. The landing gear weighed 12,000 pounds.[23]

Each main gear consisted of a main shock strut, drag braces, actuators, and a folding bogie assembly with four 40-inch diameter main wheels and 40x17.5-inch 36-ply B.F. Goodrich tires, two brakes, and a 16x4.4-inch brake reference wheel. The tires had a silver color as a result of a heat-resistant material being impregnated into the rubber during construction and also painted on the

exterior surface. The brakes were somewhat unique, with a stack of 21 stationary and 20 revolving disks located between opposing wheels and shared between them. The stationary discs were splined on a stator ring cage and the rotating discs splined to the torque tube to which the wheels were attached. The wheels ran on bearings fitted directly to the H-11 forged steel bogie instead of on an axle. Since the brake discs were separated from the wheels, much more efficient cooling was achieved. Still, at maximum effort the brake temperatures exceeded 2,000 degF and absorbed over 200 million foot-pounds of kinetic energy. An antiskid braking system was incorporated on the main gear wheels, and a small "fifth wheel" on each main bogie provided a speed reference for the antiskid system. The small fifth wheel and one main wheel contained speed sensors that

sent data to the antiskid computer. The difference in speeds between these two sensors indicated the amount of slippage (since the fifth wheel had no loads, it was assumed that it always recorded actual speed). If an excessive speed differential existed, the computer then relieved some brake pressure to that bogie.[24]

The nose gear consisted of a shock strut, drag brace, torque links, actuators, a steering servo actuator, and two 40-inch wheels and 40x17.5-inch 36-ply B.F. Goodrich tires. The nose wheels could be steered 58 degrees either side of center at taxi speeds, or 35 degrees either side of center during takeoff and landing.[25]

Three 28-foot diameter ring-slot nylon drag chutes were housed in an environmentally-controlled compartment on top of the fuselage, 18 feet from the rear of the aircraft. A 30-inch diameter spring-loaded pilot chute pulled an 11-foot diameter extraction chute which in turn deployed the three main chutes. The upward-opening compartment doors were locked in the open posi-

tion when the pilot commanded the chutes to deploy. The chutes could be deployed at speeds as high as 200 knots after the main gear was firmly on the ground.[26]

FUEL SYSTEM

Each XB-70A was equipped with 11* fuel tanks; however, since tank No. 3 was over the center-of-gravity it was used as a sump tank and not for fuel storage. Five of the tanks were located in the aft part of the fuselage neck, and three integral tanks were in the main part of each wing. Some reports indicate that AV/3 and production aircraft would have had another fuel tank in each wingtip, but the structural complexity of adding weight into this movable panel might have been extreme. On A/V-1, tank No. 5 was inoperative due to unresolved leakage problems.

The wing tanks were emptied first. From the main tanks, fuel was fed to the No. 3 sump tank as dictated by engine requirements and center-of-gravity concerns. At cruise power, fuel flowed from tank No. 3 to the engines at 785 pounds per minute. Fueling and defueling were accomplished through a single-point receptacle at a rate of 600 gallons per minute. An adjacent control panel allowed ground crew to select which tanks were to be filled or drained. A fuel tank sequence panel on the copilot's instrument panel presented a graphic display of tank sequencing. Dual-colored tapes (white and black) were used to indicate the fuel level in each tank – white indicated fuel; black indicated no fuel. When the display was completely black,

the tank was empty. The intertank transfer of fuel was automated on A/V-2, but was accomplished manually by the copilot on A/V-1. The third prototype and production aircraft would have included an aerial refueling receptacle on the upper surface of the nose forward of the articulating windshield.[27]

Fuel was used for cooling various systems through a series of heat exchangers supplied from the sump (No. 3) fuel tank. At Mach 3 the fuel could absorb over 30,000 BTUs per minute from the hydraulic, engine oil, and environmental control systems. However, towards the end of the mission or during periods when the fuel flow was low (such as during in-flight refueling when the engines were throttled back) a secondary cooling method used 4,000 pounds of water that acted as a substitute heat sink. The water was vaporized at a rate of 28 pounds per minute in a boiler by the latent heat from the systems normally cooled by the fuel.

Gaseous nitrogen was used for fuel tank pressurization and inerting. Two liquid nitrogen dewars each held 350 pounds of LN2 under 83 psi pressure. A vaporizer circuit converted the LN2 into GN2 which was then supplied to the various fuel tanks and lines under pressure. At the end of a high-speed flight, a fuel-to-water heat exchanger assured that the fuel delivered to the engines did not exceed 260 degF.[28]

Oxygen in the JP-6 was considered detrimental both to the stability of the fuel and also to aircraft safety. To help eliminate the oxygen, the fueling process for the XB-70A was somewhat elaborate. A tanker full of JP6 began by pumping the fuel into a second, empty tanker. At the same time, the second tanker was being pressurized with high-pressure dry nitrogen which was bubbled through the JP-6 as it was pumped in. The dry nitrogen drove out any oxygen in the fuel, and the "clean" JP-6 was pumped into the XB-70A already partially pressurized with nitrogen.

This was the instrumentation package installed in the weapons bay of A/V-1 on 27 July 1967. The entire package could be lowered for maintenance. The weapons bays on the two XB-70As were not functional since they could not be opened in flight and contained no suspension racks. (NASA DFRC Collection)

---

* There were 11 physical tanks; however, most technical documentation for the XB-70A says there were 8 tanks. This is because the two corresponding wing tanks were considered one logical unit since they were controlled simultaneously to maintain the center of gravity. These tanks were designed Nos. 6 left/right, 7 left/right, and 8 left/right. The fuselage tanks were designated Nos. 1 through 5.

HYDRAULIC SYSTEMS

Six airframe-mounted accessory drive system (ADS) gearboxes, each shaft-driven by a corresponding engine, were mounted in separate compartments forward of the engines. All six gearboxes drove 4,000 psi hydraulic pumps, and Nos. 2, 3, and 4 also drove ac electrical generators. The aircraft was normally powered by two generators (Nos. 3 and 4), but any of the three was capable of supplying the entire load if required. The constant-speed (8,000 rpm) generators provided 240/416-volt, 3-phase, 400 hertz power through step-down transformers. The hydraulic pumps could be run "in reverse" and were used to start the engines. Having the accessories mounted on the airframe instead of on the engine allowed easier and more rapid engine maintenance, and also eliminated building-up different engine configurations (some with ac generators; some without, etc.).[29]

The use of 4,000-psi systems instead of the customary 3,000-psi systems was an attempt to save weight, but led to a considerable number of minor problems. The 3,000-psi systems would remain the standard for the industry until the Bell V-22 introduced 5,000-psi systems in the late 1990s – again with many problems. All totaled, each XB-70A used 85 linear actuators, 50 mechanical valves, 44 hydraulic motors, and about 400 electrically-actuated solenoid valves. More than a mile of various size tubing contained 3,300 brazed and 600 mechanical joints. To avoid the large weight penalty of providing a cooling system, all of the actuators and valves were designed to withstand high temperatures.[30]

Conventional couplings were not used in the various fluid systems (hydraulic, fuel, oil) to save weight and (unsuccessfully) eliminate the possibility of leakage. Instead, all high-pressure fluid line connections were brazed; low-pressure lines were welded. North American estimated that the technique saved over 10,000 pounds.[31]

Approximately 220 gallons of a special high-temperature hydraulic fluid called "Fluid 70" (actually named Oronite 70) were used. This fluid could operate continuously at 450 degF and intermittently up to 630 degF. Although the fluid was much better than the original Oronite 8200 that had been selected, it still left much to be desired and required constant replacement due to breaking down after prolonged exposure to high temperature.[32]

ELECTRONICS

Each aircraft was equipped with two AN/ARC-90 UHF command radios that provided 3,500 channels between 225.00 MHz and 399.95 MHz, and had a built-in guard receiver tuned between 238–248 MHz. On A/V-1 only one of the UHF sets was active at a time, the other being in standby mode. On A/V-2 both sets could be used simultaneously. Antennas were located on both the top and bottom of the forward fuselage. An AN/AIC-18 intercomm allowed the two pilots to talk to each other. An AN/APX-46 transponder (IFF) set was installed on both aircraft, more for air traffic control purposes than anything else. Again, antennas were located on the top and bottom of the forward fuselage.[33]

Each XB-70A was equipped with an AN/ARN-58 instrument landing system and a standard AN/ARN-65 TACAN radio navigation system. The TACAN installation was a far cry from the sophisticated bombing-navigation system developed by IBM, and was generally considered only marginally acceptable for test flights. Without the IBM bomb-nav system, the XB-70As did not have an inertial navigation system and were forced to rely on dead-reckoning and TACAN. Fortunately, the chase planes generally had better navigation systems, and the XB-70s were always under positive radar surveillance.

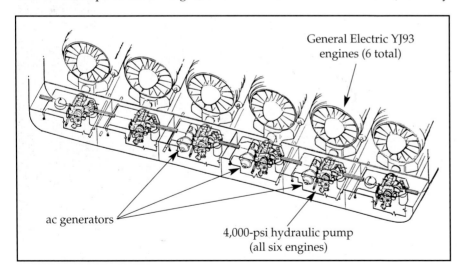

General Electric YJ93 engines (6 total)

ac generators

4,000-psi hydraulic pump (all six engines)

One of the innovations pioneered on the XB-70A was the use of airframe-mounted accessories, such as generators and hydraulic pumps. This simplified engine buildup and installation as well as logistics. (U.S. Air Force)

The central air data system provided the flight crew with displays of indicated airspeed, calibrated airspeed, indicated altitude, true altitude, Mach number, maximum safe Mach number, altitude rate (vertical velocity), indicated angle-of-attack, vertical acceleration, and total temperature. Indicated airspeed and altitude were displayed on standby indicators for both the pilot and copilot. Total temperature was displayed to the pilot. The other indications were displayed on vertical scale indicators to both pilots. Since the XB-70As were not equipped with an inertial navigation system, the acceleration data came from the flight test instrumentation package carried in the weapons bay.[34]

A 12-foot long (fuselage stations YF463 through YF605) electronic equipment compartment was located behind the crew compartment and accessed via a door in the rear of the crew compartment. The electronics compartment was pressurized and cooled, but by a separate system from that used by the crew compartment. The door between the compartments had to remained sealed except for brief periods when crew members were transiting between the compartments.[35]

Behind the electronics compartment (YF605 through YF861) was a 21-foot long environmental control equipment compartment. This compartment could also be accessed in flight through a door in the rear of the electronics compartment. Again, the compartment was pressurized and cooled by a separate system and the connecting door could not remain open for prolonged periods.[36]

GENERAL ELECTRIC J93 TURBOJET

The XB-70As were each powered by six General Electric YJ93-GE-3 turbojet engines, unofficially called the "six pack." The engine was a continuous flow gas turbine incorporating a multi-stage axial flow compressor, a fully annular combustor, a two-stage impulse reaction turbine, and an afterburner equipped with a variable area convergent-divergent exhaust nozzle. Compressor speed was governed by a hydro-mechanical fuel control with an electrical temperature override for exhaust temperature at maximum speeds.[37]

The engine was designed for continuous afterburner operation. The publicized thrust was "in the 30,000-pound class" in afterburner, but the actual figure was usually not given. In reality, the –3 engine made 28,800-lbf in afterburner at sea level. Non-afterburning performance was approximately 19,000-lbf.

The YJ93-GE-3 was 237 inches long and 52.5 inches wide; the intake was

The "six pack" of YJ93 engines in A/V-1. Note that the exhaust nozzle on engine No. 2 is open while the others are closed. The nozzles were closed using utility hydraulic power, and if no ground power was available, the last engine to be shut down (normally No. 4) would be unable to close the nozzle. (NASA DFRC Collection)

The General Electric YJ93-GE-3 engine was designed to operate in continuous afterburner. The box-like structure under the nose contained the engine's hydraulic system (separate from the aircraft systems) plus the gearbox and shaft takeoff that would drive the airframe-mounted accessories. (General Electric via the Terry Panopalis Collection)

The J93 was the first engine to use air-cooled turbine blades and also the first to use blades made from titanium alloy. This allowed operating temperatures "several hundred" degrees higher than was normal practice at the time. The blades proved somewhat more fragile than their steel counterparts, and at least 25 engines suffered foreign object debris damage during the flight test program.

42 inches in diameter. The thrust-to-weight ratio was 6:1, considered very good for the time but paling in comparison to modern turbofans. Moving most accessories to the airframe allowed for a much simpler engine installation than was traditional. An engine could be replaced in 25 minutes – a feat demonstrated on several occasions. The engine was designed to use JP-6, basically an improved kerosene derivative with improved heat stability and resistance to the formation of solids in the exhaust.[38]

Despite a protracted development effort, the YJ93-GE-3 was completed on schedule and passed its 68-hour preliminary flight rating test in 1961, in time for the original XB-70 first flight date. By the time the first aircraft was actually rolled out in Palmdale, the J93 had accumulated over 5,000 hours of test time – including 600 hours at more than Mach 2. As part of the engine test program, General Electric built a Mach 3 test facility, and also used a similar facility at the Air Force Arnold engineering Development Center in Tullahoma, Tennessee. Engine inlet tests were also conducted at AEDC, with 52 hours of tests involving 154 engine starts, 109 engine stalls, and over 200 inlet unstarts. The inlet in these tests was a 0.577-scale model using an actual small jet engine. Despite the fact that the idea had been cancelled along with the B-70 production program, the –3 engine had also been flight tested aboard a B-58 (55-0662) where it was housed in a specially-configured centerline pod. The B-58 was capable of testing the engine at Mach 2 in "real world" conditions.[39]

The No. 2 engine being removed from A/V-1. An experienced (and well-motivated) crew could change an engine in 25 minutes thanks to the large access doors and the convenience of the airframe-mounted accessory concept. Note the open exhaust on the No. 4 engine. (AFFTC History Office Collection)

The YJ93 fuel system consisted of an engine-driven, dual element, constant displacement gear-type pump that incorporated a centrifugal boost element that supplied 32 dual-orifice fuel nozzles in the main combustor. An additional 32 fuel injectors fed

the afterburner as needed. The ignition system consisted of a low-tension capacitor discharge unit that housed 4-joule and 20-joule circuits. During normal ground starts the 4-joule circuit was used; during low-temperature ground starts and for all air starts both the 4- and 20-joule systems were used.[40]

Each engine was equipped with a 3,500-psi hydraulic pump that was separate from the airframe-mounted pumps and was used only for engine control. The engine used hydraulic power to move the front and rear variable stators, and the primary and secondary exhaust nozzles.[41]

Because they were prototype engines, and the XB-70A test program was not expected to fly into known icing conditions, the engines were not equipped with anti-icing systems. However, the basic J93 design incorporated all the necessary structural facilities (internal piping for air supply, mounting pads, etc.) for an anti-icing system.[42]

The XB-70A was ahead of its time in providing a "thrust-by-wire" system. The throttle levers in the cockpit sent electrical signals to each engine control system. This in turn provided a mechanical linkage to the engine that integrated the operation of the main fuel control, afterburner fuel control, and primary nozzle area control. In addition to the conventional throttles, emergency thrust control switches were provided on the center aisle console and also in each escape capsule. Having electric control of the engines was one of the keys to providing limited aircraft control from within the sealed escape capsules, but oddly, the engine thrust could only be reduced from inside the capsule. The concept was that once the aircraft slowed

down and lost altitude, the pilots could open the capsules and control the aircraft normally.[43]

General Electric built 38 YJ93-GE-3 engines. Six were damaged beyond repair on flight 1-12, and another six were lost with A/V-2. Several others were damaged on test stands and in flight, and two were bailed to GE for use in developing the GE4 engine for the SST. A couple of the engines have been donated to museums, in addition to the six engines in A/V-1 at the Air Force Museum.[44]

After the cancellation of the J93 project, many of the lessons learned from the engine were applied to the development of the General Electric G4 turbojet designed for the Boeing Supersonic Transport (SST). The first GE4 demonstrator ran on 18 July 1966, and two days later it achieved its rated rpm. On 23 August it

achieved its design thrust of 40,000-lbf. With afterburning, the engine was to produce 52,600-lbf. A later version of the engine achieved 63,200-lbf on 19 September 1968, establishing it as the most powerful jet engine in the world at the time.[44]

MILITARY SYSTEMS

As delivered, neither XB-70A had any military systems installed, other than a non-functional weapons bay. AV/3 would have been equipped with a functional weapons bay and prototype offensive avionics. The planned capabilities were impressive, however.

The weapons bay was sized to house a multitude of bombs, including thermonuclear devices up to 10,000 pounds each, 20,000-pound conventional bombs, various smaller conventional bombs, chemical and

A YJ93 engine in a test cell at the Air Force Arnold Engineering Development Center in Tullahoma, Tennessee. Supersonic and high altitude conditions were simulated in these test cells. (General Electric via the Terry Panopalis Collection)

biological weapons, or up to two new air-to-ground missiles. The missiles were to have a range of 300–700 nm and an accuracy of less than a mile. Other missiles (probably GAM-87 Skybolts) were to be carried on external hard points under the wings, at least in some variations of the B-70.[46]

The IBM-developed AN/ASQ-28(V) bombing-navigation and missile guidance subsystem was intended to be used by both WS-110A and WS-125A before the nuclear-powered bomber was cancelled. The bomb-nav system would have incorporated a star tracker – an improvement of a unit originally intended for the Navaho intercontinental cruise missile – to allow precise navigation without the use of radio aids. At some points in its development, the ASQ-28 was to incorporate both forward- and side-looking Doppler radars – the side looking units were intended to allow relatively

"stealthy" approaches to the targets. The system was designed to be equally accurate at low level or at 2,500 knots and 100,000 feet. The search radar had a range of 200 nm, and could accurately track targets at 125 nm. A resolution of 200 feet at a range of 50 nm was expected. The avionics used various components from Goodyear (radar data processor), General Electric (X-band radar), and General Precision Laboratories (Doppler processor). At least limited testing was undertaken using C-54, RC-121, JB-29, JRB-57, and RB-66 aircraft as surrogates.[47]

As originally envisioned, the defensive avionics would consist of five elements: active and passive warning devices, threat evaluation equipment, electronic countermeasures, infrared countermeasures, and chaff dispensing rockets. Again, at least initially the systems being developed for WS-110A would also have been used on the WS-125A nuclear

aircraft. Early thought was given to adapting the AN/ALQ-27 jamming system being developed for late-model B-52s to the B-70, but the physical differences in the aircraft made this impossible. A revised system, using many of the techniques developed for the ALQ-27, was to be capable of noise jamming 30 radars simultaneously and track breaking against a further 10 simultaneous radars. It would cover virtually the entire spectrum from 50 to 16,000 megacycles. At various times, the Air Force and North American explored the application of defensive missiles, including a unique "flying saucer" design called a "lenticular defense missile" as well as more conventional designs such as modified GAR-9s. One study (SR-197) endorsed equipping these missiles with a "neutron kill" warhead that would render the enemy missile warheads inoperative without exploding them.[48]

ALERT POD

One of the more interesting systems being designed for the operational B-70 was the Alert Pod developed by Beech Aircraft. This was envisioned as a means to provide the B-70 with a self-sufficient ground power system during deployments to relatively austere bases.

One of the operational requirements laid down by SAC was that the B-70 should be ready for takeoff in less than three minutes after the crew entered the aircraft. In order to accomplish this, many of the B-70 systems would have to have already been powered-up to maintain them at correct operating temperatures. This would require external power.

The environmental control system compartment behind the crew cabin. This view is looking forward towards the cockpit. (The Boeing Company)

Instead of relying on transport aircraft to carry the external power

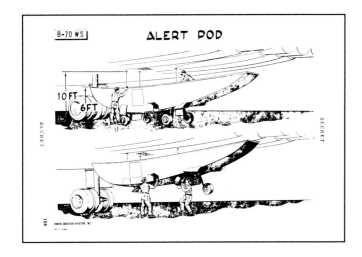

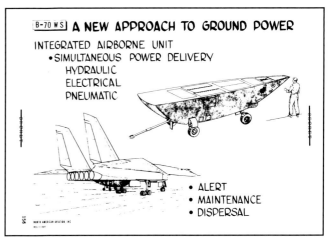

The "special power device" would have been a self-contained transportable pod that provided electrical, hydraulic, and pneumatic power. A mockup of the pod may bee see in some shots of the overall B-70 mockup, such as on page 21. The pod would have been manufactured by Beech Aircraft. (via the Jay Miller Collection)

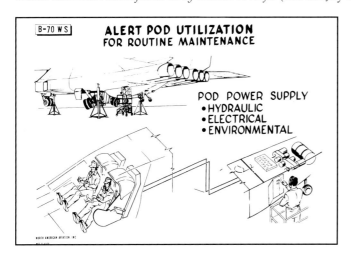

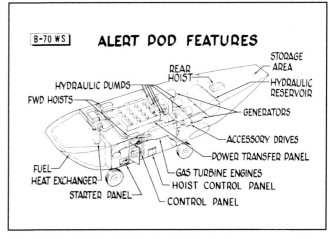

carts for the B-70, a decision was made to design all of the necessary systems into a streamlined pod that could be carried by the B-70 itself, at least during subsonic flight. The pod would provide all necessary hydraulic, electrical, and pneumatic power to the aircraft while it was on ground-alert status, and also during maintenance activities.[49]

The pod was designed to attach to the centerline of the lower fuselage behind the weapons bay, roughly under engines No. 3 and 4. The pod was equipped with its own retractable wheels that were used after it was detached from the aircraft. While sitting on its wheels, the pod was approximately 6 feet high and 30 feet long. Three built-in hoists (two at front and one rear) allowed the pod to the mated to the B-70. The pod contained two small gas turbine engines that drove six hydraulic pumps (one for each J93) and two generators. The hydraulics allowed each of the accessory drives on the B-70 to be powered in order to start the J93s. The pod could also cool and/or heat the B-70 crew compartment and equipment bays as needed. An area in the rear of the pod allowed the ground crew to store tools and minor parts, while a large JP-6 fuel tank at the front was sufficient for nine hours of unrefueled operation of the turbines. The pod could be con-

trolled locally by the ground crew, or from the crew compartment at the copilot's station.[50]

It was expected that each operational B-70 would have its own alert pod procured for it. Beech and 14 other companies submitted proposals for the pod to North American on 27 October 1958, and North American announced Beech as the winner on 23 April 1959. At the time the pod was considered highly classified and was described only as "a special power device." A mockup was inspected and approved on 1 August 1959. A prototype unit was supposed to have been completed by 1 October 1961, with production

The offensive operator's radar display for A/V-3. The left display had a film transport system and a projector to show where the B-70 "should be." The right display looked at the actual outside world, in radar format. The radar display had a recording camera on top. (Jim Tuttle Collection)

units available beginning in August 1963. But the fortunes of the B-70 project changed rapidly, and the alert pod was never completed.[51]

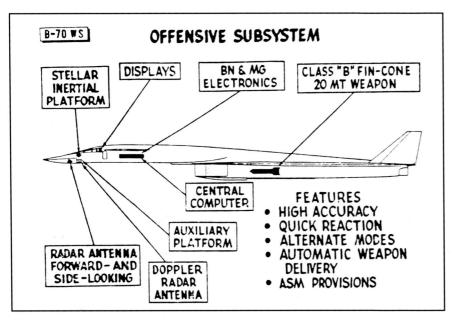

The proposed offensive systems for the B-70. The use of side-looking radar was an attempt to conceal emissions from the aircraft directly ahead. Note that a single 20 megaton thermonuclear bomb was the primary payload, although the aircraft would have been capable of carrying a variety of other nuclear and conventional gravity bombs, as well as missiles. (U.S. Air Force)

SIGNATURE REDUCTION

One of the complaints frequently voiced against the B-70 was that it was a large target. The concept of "stealth" (a term not yet applied to the idea) was not far advanced in 1960, but engineers at Lockheed and North American both understood that reducing the radar and infrared signature of strategic aircraft would at least delay their detection by the enemy. The shape and materials used by Lockheed in the Blackbird were specifically intended to lower its radar signature. Several detailed studies into the signature of the B-70 were made, and provided a basis for reduction attempts.[52]

During the very short YB-70 development period, the Air Force had directed North American to investigate means to reduce the probability the B-70 would be detected. Preliminary investigations were made into applying various radar absorbing materials (RAM) to the airframe, particularly the insides of the air intakes. However, most of the North American effort appears to have concentrated on reducing the infrared (IR) signature of the aircraft. Exhausting cool air around the J93 engines was one means of reducing the IR signature of the B-70.

As part of its research, North American actually developed a "finish system" (i.e., paint) that provided a low emittance at wavelengths used by Soviet infrared detecting devices, while radiating most of the excess heat from the surface in wavelengths not normally under surveillance. The finish utilized a low emittance basecoat with a organic topcoat that was transparent to energy in the 1 to 6 micron range. The top coating was strangely opaque and highly emissive at wavelengths

between 6 and 15 microns. This finish was relatively invisible to IR detecting equipment, while still allowing the skin to radiate excess heat overboard to maintain its structural integrity.[53]

Two different coatings were developed, one for areas that reached a maximum of 485 degF, the other for areas up to 630 degF. The first (logically, called Type I) consisted of Englehard Industries Hanovia Ceramic Metallic Coating No. 2 0.004 mils thick. Over this was applied a 1-mil thick mixture of 85 percent Ferro Enamaling No. AL-8 Frit and 15 percent Hommel No. 5933 Frit. The Type II basecoat was a mixture of 40 percent Hanovia Silver Resinate and 60 percent Hanovia L.B. Coating No. 6593 applied 0.004-mil thick. The top coat was a mixture of 74 percent 3M Kel-F No. 2140, 24 percent 3M Kel-F No. 601, and 2 percent Al2O3 applied 1-mil thick. The Type I coating was actually test flown, having been applied to one panel on the vertical

Despite the effort being cancelled when the YB-70 development program was terminated, eventually the J93 did get its ride aboard a B-58 Hustler. A special pod was created that allowed testing the J93 at Mach 2 and high altitude under real-world conditions. The single J93 added almost 50 percent to the available thrust of the B-58. (Terry Panopalis Collection)

stabilizer of the X-15 rocket plane. No observable physical changes occurred during the Mach 4.43 flight. In most probability the top coats would have been an opaque silver instead of the white finish used on the two XB-70A prototype aircraft.[54]

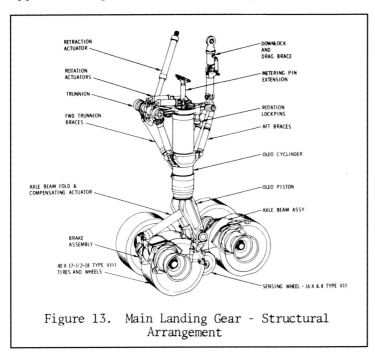

Figure 13. Main Landing Gear - Structural Arrangement

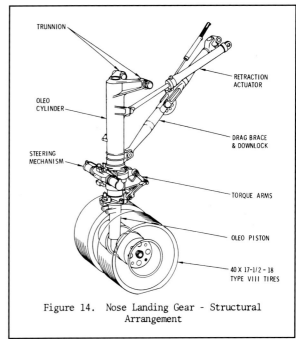

Figure 14. Nose Landing Gear - Structural Arrangement

Details of the main gear (left) and nose gear (right). All ten wheels and tires on the XB-70 were identical. (U.S. Air Force)

A new heat-reflecting tire was developed by B.F. Goodrich for the XB-70A. Here a staged photo demonstrates (by boiling water in a kettle) the tire's ability to stand the heat generated by air friction at three times the speed of sound. The tire was exposed to temperatures of 360 degF for several hours. B.F. Goodrich was awarded a patent for the heat reflective material on the tire's outer surface. (B.F. Goodrich via the Gerald H. Balzer Collection)

The finish system was somewhat difficult to apply to an aircraft as large as the YB-70s, but the engineers expected that further development would yield improvements in the process. The most difficult problem was that the underlying surface had to be highly polished prior to applying the basecoat. In addition, the basecoat of both finishes had to be cured at 750 degF, while the topcoat of the Type II finish had to be cured at 1,000 degF (creating almost a ceramic finish). Accelerated environmental tests indicated the surface would prove durable on the stainless steel sections of the aircraft, but its long-term adhesion to titanium appeared to be weak and additional work would be needed to cure this problem. Both finishes were relatively immune to exposure to hydraulic fluid, fuels, oils, and other substances expected to be encountered during operational service. Each could be readily with soap and water.[55]

[1] North American Report NA-66-901, Operational Limitations of the XB-70A Air Vehicle, prepared under NASA contract NAS4-1175, 30 August 1966. passim. [2] XB-70-2-1, Development Program Manual, General Airplane, USAF Series XB-70A Aircraft, 30 July 1966, changed 31 March 1967, p. 1-1. [3] Ibid, p. 1-2. [4] Ibid, pp. 2-2 and 2-3. [5] Ibid, p. 2-13. [6] Ibid, pp. 1-2 and 2-2. [7] Ibid, pp. 1-2, 2-15, 2-18, and 2-19. [8] "XB-70A 's Research Role will Contribute Mach 3 Flight Data for SST Development," Aviation Week & Space Technology, 18 May 1964, pp. 26-27. [9] XB-70-2-1, p. 1-1; Iain Pike, B-70 State-of-the-Art Improver, Flight International, 25 June 1964, p. 1062. [10] XB-70-2-1, pp. 1-1, 2-33, and 2-34. [11] XB-70-2-1, pp. 2-34, and 2-35; "XB-70A 's Research Role will Contribute Mach 3 Flight Data for SST Development," pp. 26-27. [12] XB-70-2-1, pp. 1-1 and 2-33. [13] Ibid, pp. 2-35 and 2-36. [14] Richard L. Schleicher, "Structural Design of the XB-70," a paper presented at the Institute of Aeronautical Sciences in 1967. [15] Ibid. [16] North American Report "XB-70 Program Engineering Effort To Be Accomplished on Contract 42058 (31 July 1962 Through 30 June 1964)," 9 August 1962; XB-70-2-1, p. 1-4. [17] XB-70-2-5, Development Program Manual (Propulsion Related Systems), USAF Series XB-70A Aircraft, 30 July 1966, changed 21 November 1966, pp.7-1 through 7-10. [18] B-70 State-of-the-Art Improver, p. 1059; "XB-70A 's Research Role will Contribute Mach 3 Flight Data for SST Development," pp. 26-27. [19] T.O. 1B-70(X)A-1, Interim Flight Manual, USAF Series XB-70A Aircraft, 31 August 1964, changed 25 June 1965; "XB-70A 's Research Role will Contribute Mach 3 Flight Data for SST Development," pp. 26-27. [20] XB-70-2-5, pp.7-1 through 7-10. [21] Ibid, pp.7-1 through 7-10; B-70 State-of-the-Art Improver, p. 1060. [22] XB-70-2-5, pp.7-1 through 7-10. [23] XB-70-2-1, pp. 1-2 and 2-17. [24] XB-70-2-1, pp. 2-16 and 2-17; B-70 State-of-the-Art Improver, p. 24. [25] XB-70-2-1, pp. 2-16 and 2-17. [26] XB-70-2-1, pp. 1-2, 2-18 and 2-19; North American Report NA-66-901, Operational Limitations of the XB-70A Air Vehicle, prepared under NASA contract NAS4-1175, 30 August 1966, p. 2; T.O. 1B-70(X)A-1. [27] XB-70-2-1, pp. 1-2, 2-8, 2-9 and 2-10. [28] XB-70-2-1, pp. 2-11 and 2-14. [29] XB-70-2-1, pp. 1-2 and 2-19. [30] "XB-70A 's Research Role will Contribute Mach 3 Flight Data for SST Development," pp. 26-27; B-70 State-of-the-Art Improver, p. 20. [31] XB-70-2-1, p. 1-1. [32] "XB-70A 's Research Role will Contribute Mach 3 Flight Data for SST Development," pp. 26-27; B-70 State-of-the-Art Improver,p. 20. [33] XB-70-2-1, pp. 2-37 and 2-38. [34] Ibid, p. 2-21. [35] Ibid, p. 1-4. [36] Ibid, p. 1-4. [37] Ibid, p. 2-3. [38] B-70 State-of-the-Art Improver, p. 1060. [39] Ibid, p. 1060. [40] XB-70-2-1, p. 2-4. [41] Ibid, p. 2-5. [42] Ibid, p. 2-6. [43] Ibid, pp. 2-6 and 2-7. [44] "NASA Assumes XB-70 Research Effort," Aviation Week & Space Technology, 13 February 1967, p. 38. [45] Jane's All the World's Aircraft, 1970-71 edition, (London: Jane's Yearbooks, 1971), pp. 765-766. [46] Development of Airborne Armament, 1910-1961, report 61WW-12808, prepared by the Air Force Systems Command, October 1961, Part I, pp. 108-160. [47] Ibid, pp. 108-160. [48] Ibid, pp. 313-380. [49] North American briefing, B-70 Weapon System Alert Pod, undated, originally classified Secret. In the Jay Miller Collection. [50] Ibid. [51] North American news release, 23 April 1959. [52] See, for example, North American Report NA-59-53-1, "Thermal Radiation Characteristics of the B-70 Weapon System," 31 July 1959 and North American Report NA-59-1887, "B-70 Radar Cross Section, Infrared Radiation, and Infrared Countermeasures," 31 December 1959. Both originally classified SECRET. [53] North American Report NA61-295 "Development of Coating Materials for Reduction of the Infrared Emission of the YB-70 Air Vehicle," 16 March 1961, originally classified SECRET. [54] Ibid. [55] Ibid.

FLIGHT LOG

The following flight log was excerpted from the XB-70 Flight Log compiled by Betty J. Love at the NASA Flight Research Center and distributed to members of the XB-70A team on 7 May 1969. The "Flt No." column identifies which aircraft and the flight number for that aircraft. The columns marked "Sub" and "Mach" identify the hours and minutes spent at each speed on each flight; the "Total Super" column is the total supersonic time (in hours and minutes) on that flight and the "Total Flight" column gives the total flight time (in hours and minutes) for the flight. The "Max Values" columns give the maximum Mach Number (Mn), speed (in mph) and altitude (in feet) for each flight.

Flt.	Date	Flt. No.	Pilot	Copilot	Sub H M	Mach 1.0–1.9	Mach 2.0–2.5	Mach 2.5–2.9	Mach 3.0	Total Super	Total Flight	Mn	mph	Feet
1	21 Sep 64	1-1	White	Cotton	1 07	- -	- -	- -	- -	- -	1 07	0.50	360	16,000
2	5 Oct 64	1-2	White	Cotton	0 55	- -	- -	- -	- -	- -	0 55	0.85	600	28,000
3	12 Oct 64	1-3	White	Cotton	1 20	0 15	- -	- -	- -	0 15	1 35	1.11	725	35,400
4	24 Oct 64	1-4	White	Cotton	0 45	0 40	- -	- -	- -	0 40	1 25	1.42	945	46,300
5	16 Feb 65	1-5	White	Cotton	0 30	0 40	- -	- -	- -	0 40	1 10	1.60	1,060	45,000
6	25 Feb 65	1-6	White	Fulton	0 53	- -	- -	- -	- -	- -	0 53	0.79	655	35,000
7	4 Mar 65	1-7	White	Fulton	0 37	1 00	- -	- -	- -	1 00	1 37	1.85	1,200	50,200
8	24 Mar 65	1-8	White	Shepard	0 26	0 34	0 40	- -	- -	1 14	1 40	2.14	1,365	56,100
9	2 Apr 65	1-9	White	Cotton	0 54	- -	- -	- -	- -	- -	0 54	0.95	630	34,500
10	20 Apr 65	1-10	White	Cotton	0 28	0 24	0 50	- -	- -	1 14	1 42	2.30	1,485	58,500
11	28 Apr 65	1-11	White	Shepard	0 27	0 19	0 57	- -	- -	1 16	1 43	2.45	1,570	64,300
12	7 May 65	1-12	White	Fulton	0 27	0 25	0 26	0 07	- -	0 58	1 25	2.60	1,690	65,000
13	16 Jun 65	1-13	White	Cotton	0 22	0 25	0 28	0 22	- -	1 15	1 37	2.60	1,700	65,000
14	1 Jul 65	1-14	White	Shepard	0 25	0 29	0 19	0 40	- -	1 19	1 44	2.85	1,900	68,000
15	17 Jul 65	2-1	White	Cotton	0 52	0 21	- -	- -	- -	0 21	1 13	1.41	935	42,000
16	27 Jul 65	1-15	White	Fulton	0 38	0 22	0 07	0 36	- -	1 05	1 43	2.82	1,900	66,000
17	10 Aug 65	2-2	Cotton	White	0 56	0 31	- -	- -	- -	0 31	1 27	1.45	950	41,000
18	18 Aug 65	2-3	Shepard	White	1 14	0 44	- -	- -	- -	0 44	1 58	1.45	950	46,000
19	20 Aug 65	2-4	Fulton	White	1 23	0 41	- -	- -	- -	0 41	2 04	1.44	950	42,000
20	17 Sep 65	2-5	White	Fulton	0 55	1 00	- -	- -	- -	1 00	1 55	1.83	1,200	50,500
21	22 Sep 65	1-16	White	Cotton	0 40	0 21	0 07	0 49	- -	1 17	1 57	2.83	1,900	67,000
22	29 Sep 65	2-6	White	Shepard	1 12	0 27	0 05	- -	- -	0 32	1 44	2.23	1,460	54,000
23	5 Oct 65	2-7	White	Shepard	1 09	0 22	0 09	- -	- -	0 31	1 40	2.30	1,520	55,000
24	11 Oct 65	2-8	White	Shepard	0 37	0 25	0 53	- -	- -	1 18	1 55	2.34	1,550	57,500
25	14 Oct 65	1-17	White	Cotton	0 37	0 24	0 22	0 22	0 02	1 10	1 47	3.02	2,000	70,000
26	16 Oct 65	2-9	White	Fulton	0 31	0 25	0 47	- -	- -	1 12	1 43	2.43	1,600	59,500
27	26 Oct 65	2-10	White	Fulton	0 56	0 28	0 43	- -	- -	1 11	2 07	2.46	1,620	59,000
28	2 Nov 65	2-11	White	Cotton	0 34	0 34	0 46	- -	- -	1 20	1 54	2.45	1,610	59,000
29	4 Nov 65	1-18	Fulton	White	0 47	1 17	- -	- -	- -	1 17	2 04	1.86	1,230	46,000
30	8 Nov 65	1-19	Cotton	White	1 37	0 46	- -	- -	- -	0 46	2 23	1.89	1,250	45,500
31	12 Nov 65	1-20	Shepard	White	1 49	0 36	- -	- -	- -	0 36	2 25	1.84	1,220	46,000
32	18 Nov 65	1-21	Cotton	Shepard	1 12	0 50	- -	- -	- -	0 50	2 02	1.88	1,240	47,000
33	29 Nov 65	2-12	White	Fulton	2 19	- -	- -	- -	- -	- -	2 19	0.53	380	15,200
34	30 Nov 65	1-22	Fulton	White	0 47	0 19	0 53	- -	- -	1 12	1 59	2.34	1,540	56,000
35	1 Dec 65	2-13	White	Fulton	0 38	0 25	0 31	0 28	- -	1 24	2 02	2.67	1,765	64,000
36	2 Dec 65	1-23	Cotton	White	0 29	0 48	0 34	- -	- -	1 22	1 51	2.46	1,620	60,000
37	3 Dec 65	2-14	White	Cotton	0 41	0 23	0 11	0 40	- -	1 14	1 55	2.87	1,900	69,000
38	7 Dec 65	1-24	Shepard	Fulton	1 46	0 18	0 22	- -	- -	0 40	2 26	2.45	1,600	62,000
39	10 Dec 65	1-25	Fulton	Shepard	1 23	0 55	- -	- -	- -	0 55	2 18	1.82	1,200	50,700
40	11 Dec 65	2-15	White	Shepard	0 47	0 23	0 12	0 41	- -	1 16	2 03	2.94	1,940	70,600
41	14 Dec 65	1-26	Shepard	Fulton	2 10	- -	- -	- -	- -	- -	2 10	0.95	670	20,000
42	20 Dec 65	1-27	Cotton	White	0 47	1 11	- -	- -	- -	1 11	1 58	1.78	1,190	42,000
43	21 Dec 65	2-16	White	Cotton	0 29	0 18	0 13	0 49	- -	1 20	1 49	2.95	1,945	72,000
44	22 Dec 65	1-28	Shepard	Cotton	2 21	0 14	- -	- -	- -	0 14	2 35	1.42	950	34,000

Flt.	Date	Flt. No.	Pilot	Copilot	Sub H M	Mach 1.0–1.9	Mach 2.0–2.5	Mach 2.5–2.9	Mach 3.0	Total Super	Total Flight	Max Mn	Values mph	Feet
45	3 Jan 66	2-17	White	Cotton	0 30	0 16	0 17	0 46	0 03	1 22	1 52	3.05	2,010	72,000
46	3 Jan 66	1-29	Fulton	Shepard	2 41	- -	- -	- -	- -	- -	2 41	0.94	655	26,000
47	6 Jan 66	1-30	Shepard	Fulton	3 40	- -	- -	- -	- -	- -	3 40	0.94	655	33,000
48	11 Jan 66	1-31	Fulton	Shepard	0 49	0 46	- -	- -	- -	0 46	1 35	1.85	1,220	46,000
49	11 Jan 66	1-32	Cotton	White	0 58	- -	- -	- -	- -	- -	0 58	0.95	650	27,000
50	12 Jan 66	2-18	White	Cotton	0 24	0 21	0 09	0 50	0 04	1 24	1 48	3.06	2,020	72,000
51	15 Jan 66	1-33	Fulton	White	0 37	0 50	- -	- -	- -	0 50	1 27	1.85	1,220	47,000
52	7 Feb 66	2-19	Shepard	Cotton	1 08	1 03	- -	- -	- -	1 03	2 11	1.44	960	42,000
53	9 Feb 66	2-20	White	Cotton	0 40	0 21	0 17	0 26	0 05	1 09	1 49	3.04	2,000	70,800
54	16 Feb 66	2-21	White	Cotton	3 04	0 02	- -	- -	- -	0 02	3 06	1.10	720	32,000
55	17 Feb 66	2-22	White	Cotton	0 24	0 18	0 15	0 35	0 15	1 23	1 47	3.04	2,000	73,000
56	26 Feb 66	1-34	Shepard	Fulton	2 22	- -	- -	- -	- -	- -	2 22	0.92	650	20,000
57	3 Mar 66	1-35	Fulton	Shepard	2 42	- -	- -	- -	- -	- -	2 42	0.55	395	15,000
58	4 Mar 66	1-36	Fulton	Shepard	1 39	0 36	0 12	- -	- -	0 48	2 27	2.02	1,330	56,000
59	7 Mar 66	1-37	Shepard	Cotton	1 17	0 46	0 16	- -	- -	1 02	2 19	2.22	1,450	57,000
60	10 Mar 66	2-23	White	Fulton	0 31	0 31	0 15	0 39	- -	1 25	1 56	2.76	1,820	67,000
61	15 Mar 66	2-24	White	Fulton	0 26	0 22	0 10	1 01	- -	1 33	1 59	2.85	1,880	69,500
62	17 Mar 66	2-25	Fulton	White	0 25	0 18	0 19	0 50	- -	1 27	1 52	2.85	1,880	70,350
63	19 Mar 66	2-26	White	Shepard	0 27	0 29	0 17	0 53	- -	1 30	1 57	2.93	1,930	74,000
64	22 Mar 66	1-38	Cotton	Shepard	2 11	- -	- -	- -	- -	- -	2 11	0.97	650	32,000
65	24 Mar 66	2-27	Fulton	White	0 45	0 18	0 10	0 19	- -	0 47	1 32	2.71	1,600	64,000
66	24 Mar 66	1-39	Shepard	Cotton	0 54	0 45	0 21	- -	- -	1 06	2 00	2.42	1,600	60,000
67	26 Mar 66	2-28	Cotton	White	3 09	- -	- -	- -	- -	- -	3 09	0.94	620	36,000
68	28 Mar 66	1-40	Shepard	Cotton	0 20	0 49	0 32	- -	- -	1 21	1 41	2.43	1,600	65,000
69	29 Mar 66	2-29	Shepard	White	0 26	1 25	- -	- -	- -	1 25	1 51	1.65	1,090	48,000
70	31 Mar 66	2-30	Shepard	White	0 50	0 18	0 12	0 50	- -	1 20	2 10	2.95	1,950	72,000
71	1 Apr 66	1-41	White	Fulton	0 54	0 55	0 20	- -	- -	1 15	2 09	2.45	1,620	58,800
72	4 Apr 66	2-31	Cotton	White	0 27	0 21	0 19	0 50	- -	1 30	1 57	2.95	1,940	73,000
73	5 Apr 66	1-42	Fulton	Shepard	0 49	0 24	0 48	- -	- -	1 12	2 01	2.43	1,600	61,000
74	8 Apr 66	2-32	Fulton	White	0 56	0 19	0 10	0 24	0 16	1 09	2 05	3.07	2,000	73,000
75	12 Apr 66	2-33	White	Cotton	0 32	0 24	0 11	0 22	0 20	1 17	1 49	3.08	2,000	72,800
76	13 Apr 66	1-43	Shepard	Cotton	0 58	0 18	0 12	0 35	- -	1 05	2 03	2.60	1,700	62,500
77	16 Apr 66	2-34	White	Cotton	0 58	0 20	0 08	0 34	0 01	1 03	2 01	3.03	2,000	71,000
78	19 Apr 66	1-44	Shepard	Fulton	1 12	- -	- -	- -	- -	- -	2 12	0.58	415	17,000
79	21 Apr 66	1-45	Shepard	Fulton	0 42	0 21	0 59	- -	- -	1 20	2 02	2.42	1,600	61,000
80	23 Apr 66	2-35	White	Cotton	0 39	0 21	0 21	0 40	- -	1 22	2 01	2.73	1,800	66,000
81	25 Apr 66	1-46	Fulton	Shepard	0 55	0 20	0 44	0 08	- -	1 12	2 07	2.55	1,680	63,000
82	26 Apr 66	2-36	Fulton	Cotton	0 48	0 27	0 39	0 11	- -	1 17	2 05	2.65	1,760	65,500
83	27 Apr 66	1-47	White	Fulton	2 33	0 08	- -	- -	- -	0 08	2 41	1.50	1,010	31,000
84	30 Apr 66	2-37	White	Cotton	2 16	- -	- -	- -	- -	- -	2 16	0.58	415	16,000
85	3 May 66	1-48	White	Fulton	1 22	- -	- -	- -	- -	- -	1 22	0.64	445	23,000
86	9 May 66	1-49	White	Fulton	2 16	- -	- -	- -	- -	- -	2 16	0.54	390	15,000
87	16 May 66	2-38	White	Cotton	0 58	0 25	0 19	0 27	- -	1 11	2 09	2.75	1,800	65,000
88	19 May 66	2-39	White	Cotton	0 28	0 18	0 11	0 29	0 33	1 31	1 59	3.06	2,000	72,500
89	22 May 66	2-40	Fulton	Cotton	1 57	0 25	- -	- -	- -	0 25	2 22	1.51	960	26,500
90	25 May 66	2-41	Shepard	Cotton	1 34	0 49	- -	- -	- -	0 49	2 23	1.63	1,065	42,000
91	27 May 66	2-42	Shepard	Cotton	0 51	0 38	0 33	0 06	- -	1 17	2 08	2.53	1,640	62,000
92	31 May 66	2-43	Shepard	Fulton	0 50	0 50	0 22	- -	- -	1 12	2 02	2.23	1,455	57,000
93	4 Jun 66	2-44	Shepard	Cotton	0 45	0 26	0 28	0 26	- -	1 20	2 05	2.93	1,930	70,000
94	6 Jun 66	2-45	Shepard	Cotton	0 45	0 22	0 12	0 32	0 09	1 15	2 00	3.05	2,000	72,000
95	8 Jun 66	2-46	White	Cross	1 59	0 14	- -	- -	- -	0 14	2 13	1.41	940	32,000
96	3 Nov 66	1-50	Cotton	Fulton	1 26	0 22	0 12	- -	- -	0 34	2 00	2.10	1,385	60,000
97	10 Nov 66	1-51	Fulton	Cotton	0 27	0 40	0 19	0 13	- -	1 12	1 39	2.52	1,660	60,000
98	23 Nov 66	1-52	Shepard	Cotton	0 32	0 44	0 13	0 09	- -	1 06	1 38	2.51	1,655	61,000
99	12 Dec 66	1-53	Fulton	Shepard	0 56	0 29	0 23	0 09	- -	1 01	1 57	2.52	1,660	60,000
100	16 Dec 66	1-54	Shepard	Fulton	0 53	0 34	0 19	0 08	- -	1 01	1 54	2.55	1,680	60,300
101	20 Dec 66	1-55	Cotton	Shepard	0 45	0 28	0 28	0 04	- -	1 00	1 45	2.53	1,640	60,800
102	4 Jan 67	1-56	Fulton	Shepard	0 47	0 22	0 27	0 08	- -	0 57	1 44	2.53	1,670	60,400
103	13 Jan 67	1-57	Cotton	Fulton	0 46	0 22	0 29	0 09	- -	1 00	1 46	2.57	1,695	61,000
104	17 Jan 67	1-58	Cotton	Shepard	0 43	0 23	0 34	0 04	- -	1 01	1 44	2.56	1,690	60,200
105	25 Jan 67	1-59	Fulton	Shepard	0 41	0 51	- -	- -	- -	0 51	1 32	1.40	930	35,000
106	31 Jan 67	1-60	Fulton	Cotton	0 43	0 49	- -	- -	- -	0 49	1 32	1.40	925	27,000

Flt.	Date	Flt. No.	Pilot	Copilot	Sub H M	Mach 1.0–1.9	Mach 2.0–2.5	Mach 2.5–2.9	Mach 3.0	Total Super	Total Flight	Max Values Mn	mph	Feet
107	25 Apr 67	1-61	Cotton	Fulton	1 07	- -	- -	- -	- -	- -	1 07	0.43	310	17,000
108	12 May 67	1-62	Fulton	Cotton	2 17	- -	- -	- -	- -	- -	2 17	0.44	315	16,500
109	2 Jun 67	1-63	Cotton	Shepard	1 41	0 42	- -	- -	- -	0 42	2 23	1.43	945	43,000
110	22 Jun 67	1-64	Fulton	Mallick	0 57	0 57	- -	- -	- -	0 57	1 54	1.83	1,205	54,000
111	10 Aug 67	1-65	Cotton	Sturmthal	2 29	- -	- -	- -	- -	- -	2 29	0.92	660	15,500
112	24 Aug 67	1-66	Fulton	Mallick	0 33	0 56	0 23	- -	- -	1 19	1 52	2.24	1,480	57,700
113	8 Sep 67	1-67	Cotton	Sturmthal	0 40	0 24	0 51	- -	- -	1 15	1 55	2.30	1,515	61,000
114	11 Oct 67	1-68	Fulton	Mallick	0 28	0 24	0 47	- -	- -	1 11	1 39	2.43	1,605	58,000
115	2 Nov 67	1-69	Cotton	Sturmthal	0 42	0 27	0 10	0 37	- -	1 14	1 56	2.55	1,680	67,000
116	12 Jan 68	1-70	Fulton	Mallick	0 53	0 19	0 13	0 29	- -	1 01	1 54	2.55	1,685	67,000
117	13 Feb 68	1-71	Mallick	Cotton	2 27	- 16	- -	- -	- -	0 16	2 43	1.18	780	41,000
118	28 Feb 68	1-72	Fulton	Sturmthal	1 51	- -	- -	- -	- -	- -	1 51	0.41	295	18,500
119	21 Mar 68	1-73	Cotton	Fulton	2 32	- -	- -	- -	- -	- -	2 32	0.29	310	15,500
120	11 Jun 68	1-74	Mallick	Fulton	1 11	- -	- -	- -	- -	- -	1 11	?	?	9,500
121	28 Jun 68	1-75	Sturmthal	Cotton	2 21	0 18	- -	- -	- -	0 18	2 39	1.23	810	39,400
122	19 Jul 68	1-76	Mallick	Fulton	1 07	0 48	- -	- -	- -	0 48	1 55	1.62	1,070	42,000
123	16 Aug 68	1-77	Fulton	Sturmthal	1 00	0 21	0 34	- -	- -	0 55	1 55	2.47	1,630	63,000
124	10 Sep 68	1-78	Mallick	Fulton	0 44	0 29	0 35	- -	- -	1 04	1 48	2.50	1,650	62,800
125	18 Oct 68	1-79	Sturmthal	Fulton	1 02	0 41	0 13	- -	- -	0 54	1 56	2.18	1,440	52,000
126	1 Nov 68	1-80	Sturmthal	Fulton	1 20	0 48	- -	- -	- -	0 48	2 08	1.62	1,070	41,000
127	3 Dec 68	1-81	Fulton	Mallick	1 02	0 56	- -	- -	- -	0 56	1 58	1.64	1,080	39,400
128	17 Dec 68	1-82	Fulton	Sturmthal	0 33	0 31	0 27	0 14	- -	1 12	1 45	2.53	1,670	63,500
129	4 Feb 69	1-83	Fulton	Sturmthal	3 17	- -	- -	- -	- -	- -	3 17	0.92	625	29,000

Total Flight Time for both air vehicles: 145 28 55 50 28 41 20 51 1 48 107 10 252 38

Air Vehicle No. 1 logged 160 hours and 16 minutes during 83 flights
Air Vehicle No. 2 logged 92 hours and 22 minutes during 46 flights

Flight Hours By Pilot

Name	Affiliation	# Flights Pilot	# Flights Copilot	Sub H:M	Mach 1.0–1.9	Mach 2.0–2.4	Mach 2.5–2.9	Mach 3.0	Total Flight
Mr. Alvin White	North American Aviation	49		44 32	17 25	11 47	13 16	1 23	123 33
			18	18 22	10 42	2 37	3 13	0 16	
Colonel Joseph Cotton	United States Air Force	19		24 37	7 35	3 37	1 44	- -	119 30
			43	43 32	17 40	8 50	10 23	1 32	
Mr. Van Shepard	North American Aviation	23		30 19	12 00	5 01	2 46	0 09	95 50
			23	25 24	10 25	6 59	2 47	- -	
Fitzhugh "Fitz" Fulton	(total of USAF and NASA)	31		35 48	15 30	7 28	3 05	0 16	124 25
			32	40 46	11 34	6 50	3 08	- -	
Lt. Colonel Fitzhugh Fulton	United States Air Force	16		18 22	7 59	4 18	2 01	0 16	76 49
			22	28 41	7 14	4 59	2 59	- -	
Mr. Fitzhugh Fulton	Flight Research Center	15		17 26	7 31	3 10	1 04	- -	47 36
			10	12 05	4 20	1 51	0 09	- -	
Mr. Donald Mallick	Flight Research Center	4		5 29	1 33	0 35	- -	- -	16 54
			5	3 53	3 32	1 23	0 29	- -	
Lt. Colonel Emil Sturmthal	United States Air Force	3		4 43	1 47	0 13	- -	- -	21 51
			7	10 32	1 43	2 02	0 51	- -	
Major Carl Cross	United States Air Force	0		- -	- -	- -	- -	- -	2 13
			1	1 59	0 14	- -	- -	- -	

A PILOT'S PERSPECTIVE

Air Vehicle (A/V) No. 1 was delivered to the flight test department on 10 May 1964. For the next three months certain manufacturing items were completed, systems received operational evaluations, and Phase I proof load tests were conducted. North American and Air Force inspections were completed on 7 August 1964. The first three taxi tests were conducted on 9, 16, and 24 August, and were considered unsatisfactory due to hydraulic line failures. Repairs were undertaken overnight, and a successful taxi test (the fourth) was performed on 25 August. Two additional taxi tests (5 and 6) were conducted on 14 September, and first flight occurred on 21 September 1964.[1]

The XB-70A represented a significant departure in both design and performance from other aircraft of its era. One of the frequent questions is "how did it fly?" It seems easier to let one of the pilots that flew it answer that question. It must be remembered that the two air vehicles that were built were not representative of an operational aircraft – many systems were either not installed, not thoroughly tested, or were placeholders for advanced systems that were cancelled when the aircraft were relegated to test vehicles. The remainder of this appendix is excerpted from North American NA-66-1138, <u>XB-70A Flight Test Summary Report, Contract AF33(657)-12395</u>, prepared in late 1966 but never published. A few typographic errors, misspellings and the like have been corrected, and the meaningless (for this use) official paragraph numbers have been deleted, but otherwise it is taken directly from the report.

"This section summarizes pilot opinion of flying the XB-70A. All comments herein were extracted directly from XB-70A PILOTS SUMMARY REPORT written by Mr. A. S. White, Chief Test Pilot. Detailed PILOT FLIGHT REPORTS may be found in the North American FLIGHT TEST MONTHLY PROGRESS REPORTS, NA-66-360-1 through NA-66-360-23.

<u>Summary:</u> The XB-70A has proven itself to be a very remarkable airplane. It has accomplished every milestone that was set down for it. No aerodynamic changes were required in order to achieve the objectives but in spite of its tremendous performance, the XB-70A is an unfinished airplane. It was operated in a completely new speed and altitude range, but with off-the-shelf navigation equipment and flight instrumentation that were obsolete for this type of flight operation. This pilot believes that with normal development, including some aerodynamic refinement, some system changes, and better instruments navigational equipment, this would be a truly outstanding airplane.

<u>General:</u> In reading this pilot's summary report, consideration should be given to the fact that the combination of this airplane's size, weight, and speed ranges compares to no other airplane in existence; and that the program was primarily a research program with ground rules that allowed only those changes which were necessary to safely accomplish the test objectives. In the normal sequence of development to an operational airplane, many of the opinions and recommendations expressed herein would have been made after the initial airworthiness flights. They are presented now, for the record, and for consideration if improvements can be made for follow-on programs.

In general terms the XB-70A vas an interesting airplane to fly. It had some peculiarities due to size, weight, and configuration that were different from most other airplanes. The movable tips introduced some new characteristics in the airplane that had not been experienced before, such as the wide variation in directional stability, roll power, and dihedral effect.

The airplane had a tremendous performance capability and was a thrill to fly from that standpoint, but this capability combined with the fact that the airplane was climbed and cruised very near the boundary of the allowable flight envelope quicker and easier than any other airplane this pilot has flown. The duct pressure limits and the low allowable "g" aggravated the recovery. All this adds to the pressure on the pilot by requiring greater concentration on his part. This was acceptable in a research program of this nature, but would certainly not be acceptable in an operational vehicle. The potential for a great airplane is here but some refinements are required. More specifically, the pilot's opinions and recommendations are as follows:

<u>Ground Handling Qualities:</u> Taxiing the airplane was not a difficult operation. Turns from one narrow taxiway to another narrow taxiway was made with acceptable accuracy. However, parking the airplane in a precise location was difficult because of the restricted visibility, configuration of the airplane, and lack of repeatability of the nosewheel steering system, i.e., the nosewheel steering rate varied with the load on the nose gear so that full rudder pedal application did not consistently give the same turning rate. Ground observers were required for parking, but their inputs were sometimes valueless due to the steering system's inability to follow their directions. *Cooper Rating of 3.5*

Originally the braking system was unsatisfactory at very low speeds, but with development, the system became marginally satisfactory. The airplane could be stopped without brake chatter as long as the pilot anticipated far enough in advance to be able to apply very light braking to make the stop. If an abrupt stop was required at low speeds, heavy brake chatter occurred. *Cooper Rating 4.5*

<u>Low Speed In-Flight Handling Qualities:</u> The pitch control in low speed flight regime was very good. Some lack in airplane response could be detected during abrupt pitch maneuvers; however, the response was satisfactory in all of the normal maneuvers used in flying the airplane. The long period of the short-period oscillation was different from most other airplanes, but did not cause difficulty in controlling the airplane. The damping in pitch was good in the subsonic flight regime. *Cooper Rating of 2.5*

The main difficulty in flying the XB-70A was caused by a combination of characteristics in the lateral-directional sense. These characteristics were: First, that the period of the short-period oscillation was very long as compared to most other airplanes, secondly, the side force per degree of sideslip was low in this airplane. This combination made it difficult for the pilot to sense inadvertent sideslips. In addition to those characteristics, the airplane had a marked positive dihedral effect (particularly A/V2) and it had excessive adverse yaw due to ailerons. Considering these four characteristics together, if an inadvertent sideslip occurred without the pilot's knowledge (busy with other system's operation), the airplane rolled due to the dihedral effect. Instinctive reaction of the pilot was to coun-

teract the roll with aileron; however, the aileron input increased the sideslip because of the high adverse yaw due to aileron This increased sideslip caused more roll away from the aileron input and aggravated the situation. The solution was that the pilot had to fly the sideslip or yaw indicator religiously throughout the flight regime. This general characteristic of the XB-70A was most predominant with the wing tips up. *Cooper Rating of 4.5*

Placing the wingtips in the one-half position reduced the tendency for the situation explained in the previous paragraph, because lowering the wingtips reduced the roll power by approximately 50%, therefore reducing yaw due to aileron. In addition, the tips down configuration reduced the positive dihedral effect. *Cooper Rating of 4.0*

The longitudinal trim system was very good. *Cooper Rating of 2.0*

The lateral trim system was also very good, except that the primary lateral trim control was difficult to operate with a high degree of accuracy when the pilot was wearing heavy gloves. *Cooper Rating of 3.0*

The directional trim system was very good after the gear had been retracted. It was too sensitive with the gear down, which caused the pilot to over control when attempting to trim out directionally. Occasionally some difficulty was encountered when engaging the nosewheel steering system due to the inability of finding the neutral directional trim position.

For instance, the pilot would trim out directionally prior to putting the gear down; however, the trim system would not be exactly centered at this time. When the gear was lowered, this minor out-of-trim condition was amplified by a ratio of four to one. Due to turbulence and low speed flight characteristics, this out-of-trim condition would go undetected until after landing when the rudders were released and the nosewheel steering engaged which resulted in an abrupt transient in the steering system. It was recommended that consideration e given to reducing the directional trim rate and incorporating a rudder position indicator. *Cooper Rating of 3.0*

The compatibility of the roll and pitch force gradients was satisfactory; however, due to the large differences in the moments of inertia, the airplane responded much quicker in roll than in pitch or yaw. This was not considered to be a discrepancy against the airplane, but a characteristic of

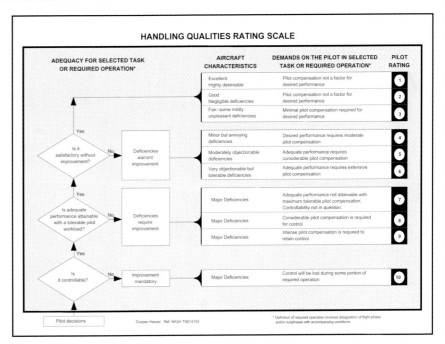

The Cooper-Harper scale is a standard method of measuring the pilot workload of an aircraft. A low score is good; a high score is bad. For the most part Al White rated the aircraft towards the low end of the scale. Given that it was a prototype vehicle, this is a tribute to its basic design. If the aircraft would have entered production, it would have been improved. (NASA)

a very long and narrow configuration. It required some getting use to by the pilots in order not to over control in roll, particularly with the tips up. A change should not be made in the response characteristics, but something should be done to reduce the adverse yaw due to ailerons. This would eliminate the primary objectionable characteristics in the airplane. If the pilots were not concerned about generating yaw with aileron inputs, the fighter-like roll response would not be objectionable. Control force compatibility *Cooper Rating of 3.0*

The trim change while operating the landing gear was negligible. The trim change while operating the wing tips was small and occurred at such a slow rate that it was hardly noticeable to the pilot since he took care of it in the normal trimming of the airplane. The trim change due to operation of the flaps was large, but easily manageable with the trim system. Although the trim system did take care of the trim change, when the flaps were lowered the control column moved very near the forward end of its travel leaving very little usable down elevon for maneuvering, go-around, or flying in turbulent air. This could be extremely hazardous in the instance where the CG was farther aft than normal.

It was recommended that a design change be made whereby more down elevon control would be available with flaps down.

The airplane had moderate buffet at low speeds with the gear and flaps down. There was a minor change in the buffet level as the gear and flaps were raised. Some buffet persisted and a high aerodynamic noise level existed until the airplane accelerated to 0.87 Mn or above, at which time the buffet completely disappeared and the noise was reduced to at least half of the low-speed level.

<u>High Speed In-Flight Handling Qualities</u>: Pitch control during the transonic acceleration and low supersonic speed ranges was very good. Above Mach 2.0 it became evident that there was some deterioration in the effectiveness of the pitch control. At speeds above 2.5 Mn, the force level required to maneuver the airplane was excessive due to this deterioration and due to the action of the "g" bellows. *Cooper Rating of 3.5*

The directional control was adequate to take care of three engines out on one side, but was much less effective in producing yaw than were the ailerons. Considering the

A TB-58A flies chase on A/V-2. The B-58 did not make a great chase aircraft since visibility was somewhat limited and maintenance expenses were high. However, it was one of the few Mach 2 aircraft that could stay airborne for any length of time in the days before aerial refueling was commonly used to support flight test programs. (Rockwell via the Jay Miller Collection)

capability of the rudders alone, they were considered adequate. Cooper Rate of 3.0. However, the powerful capability of the ailerons in producing yaw was considered the most objectionable characteristic in the airplane. *Cooper Rating of 4.5*

The roll response of the airplane in the supersonic flight regime was good. The roll response did not seem to deteriorate at the same rate as pitch response, and therefore there was less compatibility in the response of the airplane between Mach 2.0 and 2.7 than in other areas. As the airplane approached Mach 3, the roll response deteriorated and the yaw due to aileron input was reduced; therefore the handling qualities of the airplane in roll were better at Mach 3 than at any other supersonic speed. *Cooper Rating for the roll control system was 3.5*

Although there were minor differences in the flight characteristics between Mach 1.4 and Mach 3 with all augmentation off, the general characteristics were the same. The short-period oscillations in pitch and yaw were 4 to 6 seconds in length and the damping in pitch and yaw was relatively poor. The airplane could be flown at all speeds with the augmentation off, except that extreme care had to be used in the use of ailerons because of the strong tendency to excite lateral-directions oscillations with the ailerons. This was due to a high roll rate in the unaugmented case and because of the excessive level of yaw due to ailerons. When the pilots left the ailerons alone, the yawing oscillations would

damp. *Unaugmented supersonic flight Cooper Rating of 5.0*

In-Flight Visibility: The visibility with the windshield down was satisfactory. Although some forward visibility was lost after the rotation at takeoff and during the initial part of the climbout, the remainder of the subsonic flight was satisfactory. The visibility for landing was considered good. At no time was the pilot aware of any loss of the runway visibility during approach, flare, and touchdown: *Cooper Rating of 3.0*

Visibility with the windshield in the up position was unsatisfactory. The pilot cannot see the horizon ahead and must make the flight almost entirely with reference to the pitch attitude indicating system and the poor quality of the heading information precise heading, climb schedule, and altitude flying were extremely difficult. In addition images of light-colored ground such as snow and sandy desert areas reflected badly in the windshield during turns, at times causing vertigo. *Cooper Rating of 5.0*

In-Flight Unstarts: The inadvertent inlet unstarts encountered in the flight test program varied in intensity from mild to severe. They were breathtaking to say the least. In the case of a severe unstart, it jarred the airplane rather violently and was followed by heavy buffeting, intense aerodynamic noise, and minor trim changes. At Mach 3, the primary trim change was in roll, but usually did not persist since the other inlet would normally unstart within a

few seconds. If the inlet system did not effect an immediate restart, the inlet would go into buzz. The buzz cycle was immediately recognizable to the pilot since it was almost purely a lateral oscillation at about the natural frequency of the fuselage. If it was not corrected, it built up in intensity to a very disturbing, if not destructive magnitude. In spite of the severity of the transients caused by inlet unstarts airplane control was considered good.

Landing: The X-70 was not a difficult airplane to land. Some care had to be used due to the distance between the pilot and the main gear and due to the crew station height above the main gear at touchdown. Because of these dimensions, it was easy to undershoot the runway. After some practice, all pilots were able to make satisfactory landings without external assistance from chase aircraft.

The wing of the XB-70A experienced a strong ground effect in the proximity of the runway which helped considerably in making relatively smooth landings. The secret to a good landing, like in most airplanes, was a good stabilized approach using a rather low rate of descent (2 to 3 degrees glide scope).

Cross wind landings in the XB-70A were not as difficult as was predicted. The relatively shallow bank angle per degree of sideslip made the wing-down technique rather easy to use with the XB-70.

Landing in turbulent air required additional pilot concentration, primarily due to previously mentioned relationship between inadvertent sideslip, dihedral effect, and yaw due to ailerons. The pilot was required to watch the yaw indicator very closely in making an approach so as not to get into this inadvertent sideslip condition close to the ground. *Cooper Rating was 3.5*

Escape Capsule: The pressure seals in the capsule doors were torn loose many times when the pilots entered the capsules. Entering the capsule, particularly when wearing the pressure suit, was very difficult due to the lack of space. The seals should be guarded so that they are not damaged in this way.

The original installation of the capsule handgrip seat pins included a lanyard and a take-up reel which were installed behind the pilot's shoulder. A large percentage of the time the take-up reel did not operate; and when it did operate, the pin was extremely hard to reach to reinstall after flight. A temporary fix was made by cutting

the lanyard, thereby eliminating the take-up reel. This worked satisfactorily, except for the minor inconvenience of not having a place to stow the pin.

The emergency parachute and riser cutter handles and the hinge split handle were difficult to see when encapsuled. When the pilot raised his head to see the handles with his helmet on, he had to raise his helmet with his hand in order to see past the bow of the helmet. This was particularly true when the pilot was wearing a pressure suit and was aggravated under the dynamic conditions encountered after ejection.

The pressurization and capsule oxygen gages were particularly hard to see once in the capsule. The safety belt was almost impossible to adjust after it had been fastened. The seal deflate button was very difficult to actuate due to its location when the pilot was wearing a pressure suit.

The hot mike interphone capability during encapsulation was operable only after the capsule doors were closed. It appears wise, after the experience of the recent ejection, at the hot mike be actuated in another way in addition to the door closure. It should be connected to the handgrips so that when encapsulation is made, the hot mike interphone is available even if the doors are not closed. [this refers to the fact that the microphone was not hot while Carl Cross was trying to eject, so no record of what happened was available to the crash investigators]

The manual impact attenuator inflation device was extremely difficult to get to while encapsulated. It was recommended that some thought be given to relocating this device between the pilot's knees for easier access.

The Secondary Nozzle Rheostat: This rheostat is in a poor location considering the number of times it was used during flight. It would be desirable to move it forward in the area near the oxygen and visor heater switches.

Hydraulic Pump Status Indicators: The hydraulic pump status indicators became almost useless in view of the number of times the pump status indicators showed yellow with the pumps operating properly.

Nosewheel Steering System: The nosewheel steering engage button ideally should be mounted on the control wheel. Originally this was not done because of lack of space on the wheel. The pilots believed that the

augmentation disengage switch should have the priority location on the wheel. The experience gained in the flight test program indicates that it would be satisfactory to move the augmentation disengage switch to the same area as the augmentation engage button on the console and put the nosewheel steering engage switch on the control wheel.

TACAN: The TACAN instrumentation on the XB-70A was only marginally satisfactory. Early in the program the pilots were requested to list the minimum equipment with which they could accomplish the mission, and one TACAN was suggested for navigation. Experience has now shown that without radar tracking and the occasional assistance of the FAA centers, some of the missions would have been extremely difficult to complete satisfactory due to the quality of this equipment and installation.

Attitude and Heading Information: The attitude and heading information were marginally satisfactory. This added to the pilots difficulty in navigating the airplane. In view of the above two conditions, it was highly desirable to have a more reliable navigation system. An inertial platform was highly recommended.

AICS Controls: The AICS controls were satisfactory for the development stages, although the controls in A/V1 were minimally satisfactory. It was highly recommended that this system be reviewed for future use.

Flaps: The flap system was marginally satisfactory. Because of a design problem, the flaps were to be raised for the taxi and lowered just prior to takeoff in order to ensure that they would retract in flight. Occasionally they would not extend for landing, and occasionally they would not retract after landing. The result was that the pilots lost confidence in the flap system. It was recommended that a design change be made to eliminate the necessity of the intricate procedure that was required to operate the flap system.

Map Case: The map case was almost inaccessible to the pilots. In most cases the pilot had to get out of his seat to get the equipment from the map case. Although the map case was of little use to the pilots, it was the only place in the cockpit that extra material could be stored. Check lists and pilots data cards had to be strapped to the pilots legs to be of any use. Some consideration should be given to a more convenient stowage space for let-down charts, handbook, and additional maps, particularly if this airplane is to be used for cross-country work in the future.

Wingtip-Selector Switch: If the flaps are lowered for landing prior to raising the wingtips to the up position, it would be possible to lose control of the airplane. It was recommended that a safety device be installed to prevent lowering the flaps when the tips were not in the up position.

In order to suppress some noise during engine runups, North American built a set of "mufflers" that could be attached to the rear of the aircraft, covering three J93 exhausts at a time. The muffler can be seen in the background at right. This is A/V-2 taxing at Edwards. (AFFTC History Office Collection)

[1] North American Report NA-66-1138, XB-70A Flight Test Summary report, Contract AF33(657)-12395, prepared in late 1966 but never published, p. 1-5.

ALKYLBORANE

Since the creation of the internal combustion engine, hydrocarbons had been the chosen fuels because of cost, availability, and convenient physical properties. The search more efficient fuels found the improvement potential of existing hydrocarbons exhausted – or apparently so. But adapting piston power plants to use something other than hydrocarbon fuels was judged to be too difficult. The jet engine, however, seemed to offer new possibilities.

After preliminary investigations by several companies, the use of high energy fuels (HEF) in air-breathing turbojets seemed a likely possibility. Numerous special fuels were considered. Metal slurries – particularly magnesium – and liquid hydrogen* received some attention, but alkylborane fuels† were believed to have the greatest promise. Weighing approximately the same as conventional fuels and occupying about the same volume, the boron-based fuels were expected to produce 40 percent more energy than JP-4. It appeared that alkylborane products could serve as the only propellant or as additives to standard fuels. Their use could also be limited to only the afterburner (considered the easiest immediate implementation) or they could be used in the primary combustor, although this approach would take a complete reevaluation of the hot-section of the engine.

The high energy fuels promised a 16-percent range improvement over an all-JP-4 mission when the new fuels were used only in the afterburners. With engines using boron fuels in both the primary combustor and afterburner, a range improvement of 30 percent seemed feasible.

Despite the seemingly promising preliminary studies, in mid-1955 the WADC did not have a specific program directed toward using high energy fuels in the primary combustor. The Power Plant Laboratory had conducted some experiments using boron fuels in representative afterburners, but a lack of sufficient quantities of the fuels for useful testing led the laboratory to abandon the trials. Only General Electric gave any indication of serious interest in high energy fuel afterburner development; Pratt & Whitney stated that it had no interest in alkylborane fuels until more of the problem areas were defined and resolved.[1]

The confusing definition of the WS-110A and WS-125A systems had led to a "strong requirement" for some sort of range extension, and boron fuels seemed to offer a relatively easy solution. Although they would require a largely new infrastructure, including a dedicated tanker fleet, they would allow the new bombers to conduct their final refueling well outside Soviet airspace, and require fewer tankers for each mission. On the surface, it seemed so simple.

It wasn't. During the early 1950s, nobody had the capability to produce the alkylborane fuels in large quantity. The WADC observed that the development of a HEF engine depended on a successful development of an alkylborane fuel production infrastructure. A small pilot plant was under construction and would be producing 0.8 tons per day by mid-1957, with production rising to 25 tons per day over the next two years. Facilities needed $8 million in FY56, with an additional $12 million required for each of the three succeeding years. To purchase high energy fuels from these plants the WADC asked for $3.9 million and $7.8 million in FY56 and FY57, respectively.[2]

The WADC predicted that adequate fuel production could lead to development of a qualified afterburner in three years. However, it was pointed out that there was no budgetary provision to apply high energy fuels to an engine for a particular program, such as WS-110A or WS-125A.

This new military interest in boron fuels spurred development in a relatively unknown field since boron chemistry was very complex and differed considerably from other fields of chemistry. General Electric was one of the first companies to conduct an investigation of boron compounds as special fuels, beginning in the mid-1940s. About the same time, the Navy Bureau of Aeronautics also began studying boron hydrides. It was not until 1952, however, that Bureau of Aeronautics launched a boron fuel program – Project ZIP* conducted by the Callery Chemical Corporation and the Olin Mathieson Chemical Corporation. Callery began producing small amounts of a alkylborane – called ethyldecaborane – in November 1953. Meanwhile, GE was continuing its research as a subcontractor to Olin Mathieson.

The Air Force awarded a $178,000 contract (AF33(616)-2961) to General Electric for a small-scale fuel evaluation known as Project DASH to determine the thermodynamic characteristics of boron oxide exhaust products. The first major effort to extrapolate these small-scale laboratory studies to an actual engine was Project ZOOM conducted by General Electric under contract AF33(616)-3367. This project included modifying a J79-type afterburner to run on either JP-4 or HEF-3 during ground tests. A limited number of flight tests were also conducted using a modified J57 afterburner in a McDonnell F-101 Voodoo.

Although General Electric's early research was somewhat hampered by a lack of fuel, by the end of 1957 they had concluded that the use of high energy fuel in the afterburner of an engine was feasible. This early work accomplished considerable advances in useful materials, definition of design problem areas, fuel properties, and new data on exhaust products and thermodynamics.

The tactical and strategic values of the new fuels were apparent, but such serious problems as the production of fuels, predicted handling difficulties, and high production costs impeded their utilization. Basic research also revealed that one of the most critical problems in burning boron fuels was the formation of boron oxide† deposits that proved to be an excellent flux for certain metal oxides, limiting the construction materials that could be used. The solid and liquid exhaust products, however, could be quite deleterious to the working components of high performance engines and could greatly reduce operating efficiency and longevity.

In March 1957 the WADC presented a high energy fuel evaluation program to Air Force Headquarters. This plan emphasized the development of a turbojet with an afterburner that used the new fuel. Significantly, the program was oriented around requirements to support WS-110A. The WADC expected to create a qualified afterburner in 1962 and a main combustor in 1963.[3] Air

---

* Lockheed spent considerable time on the development of a hydrogen-powered aircraft under Project SUNTAN.
† The eventual boron-based high energy fuels included: HEF-1, ethyldiborane; HEF-2, propylpentaborane; HEF-3, ethyldecaborane; HEF-4, methyldecaborane; HEF-5, ethylacetylenedecaborane.

Force Headquarters accepted this program, although its response stressed that the application of high energy fuel to a particular weapon system engine (even for the WS-110A) was not a requirement.[4]

Soon after North American became the weapon system contractor in late 1957, the B-70 Project Office reiterated its belief that HEF-3 was the most economical method to achieve the desired 15-percent range increase over an all JP-4 mission. Largely to satisfy these problems, GOR 82 was revised on 7 March 1958 to include a study of "all methods of range extension" to achieve an unrefueled range of 11,000 nm.[5] The tentative operational concept alluded to the use of "high energy fuels" at a time (May 1958) when their was no formal development program in place for such an engine. One problem was that the higher temperatures created by the fuels further complicated the development of materials for use in afterburner and nozzle fabrication. Surprisingly, high energy fuel never became a specific requirement for the B-70 program, although the use of HEF-3 in the afterburner and the resultant dual-fuel capability to handle JP-4 and HEF-3 did become an integral part of the early B-70 design.

On 28 May 1958 the ARDC asked for authority to pursue the development of a high energy fuel afterburner for the J93 engine. Air Force Headquarters agreed on 10 June that the new fuel was potentially the best method of significant range improvement and directed that the basic B-70 airframe would incorporate, to the maximum degree feasible, the necessary provisions for using an engine capable of using the new fuel. On 12 February 1959 General Electric was authorized to begin development of the J93-GE-5 engine with the same basic airflow and speed characteristics as the –3, but equipped with an afterburner capable of burning either JP-4 or HEF-3.[6]

The development of new alloys or resistant coatings was imperative. The Materials Laboratory at the WADC, the NASA Lewis Research Center, General Electric, Pratt & Whitney, Marquardt, Curtiss-Wright, the Navy's Bureau of Aeronautics, Johns Hopkins University, the International Nickel Company, Fairchild, Allison, Reaction Motors, Firth Sterling, Incorporated, and two divisions of the Union Carbide Corporation (the Haynes Stellite Company and the Linde Company) held numerous meetings in 1958 to solve this fundamental problem. The results of these consultations indicated that an alloy could probably be developed for unstressed engine components operating at temperatures up to 2,300 degF, and a silicon bearing or silicate refractory coating for temperatures over 2,300 degF.[7]

These inquiries also established that most metallic materials had little effect upon HEF-3, although some lead and copper alloys could catalyze fuel decomposition. The fuel's effects on metallic materials presented no problems, but nonmetallic materials – particularly elastomers – were another question. Perhaps even more disturbing, HEF-3 was ten times as toxic as cyanide, necessitating the development of special handling and storage techniques. This toxicity also raised questions regarding the fuel's use by operational military units, but it was expected that methods could be found to mitigate the hazard. The low spontaneous ignition temperature required a nitrogen atmosphere in all ullage areas of the fuel tanks, as well as a nitrogen purge of all empty fuel tanks and lines.

The heating value of the HEF-3 fuel was more than 25,000 BTUs per pound, compared to the 18,000 of JP-4 and a bit over 26,000 BTUs for HEF-4. The spontaneous ignition temperature of the high energy fuel was about 2,600 degF, against 4,550 for JP-4, explaining the necessity for fuel system purging.

The HEF-3 fuel tended to solidify after a time at high temperatures, and the presence of moisture and oxygen accelerated this decomposition; however, bulk fuel in airframe tanks would probably not reach temperatures high enough for thermal decomposition to become a problem. Little additional thermal decomposition would occur when the fuel passed through high temperature zones in the fuel system, but residual fuel that remained in tanks or stood idle in fuel systems could easily reach solidification temperature in a short time. In flight flushing of tanks, pumps, and fuel systems with JP-4 was a possible answer, requiring that the two fuels be compatible.

While petroleum fuels required relatively simple refining operations, crude boron mixtures had first to be manufactured from basic chemicals before they could be refined. These extra steps imposed a substantial cost penalty on production of high energy fuels, and the additional electric power required further increased costs. One estimate held that a 10 tons-per-day production facility to support one B-70 wing with HEF-3 would cost $35 million to build.

By the time the B-70 became operational, high energy fuel production costs per pound could be reduced to $1.50 or so, still very much higher than JP-4 at $0.02 per pound (about ten cents a gallon). However, in terms of performance gains, the new fuels could be justified.[8]

Several companies carried on high energy fuel research. This plural contracting broadened the investigation but impeded the focusing of research on problems most pertinent to WS-110A. In order to provide better guidance, the "HEF Guidance Committee" was formed in September 1958 with members from the WADC, ARDC, Olin Mathieson, General Electric, North American, and NASA.

On 12 February 1959 Richard E, Homer, Assistant Secretary of the Air Force for Research and Development, called for a change in special-fuel priorities from the B-70 to the Bomarc missile. Suggesting that there was an "apparent need" to study further the application of high energy fuel to the B-70, Homer recommended a delay in the construction of additional fuel production facilities.[9]

SAC's reaction to this recommendation was emphatic. General Power urged on 25 March 1959 that no action be taken to divert high energy fuel priorities pending the completion of studies his command was making on the subject. He commented that it would certainly be unwise to interrupt the program at the very time it was gaining momentum from developmental successes. General Power also averred that the use of high energy or JP-4 in the B-70 engine afterburner had always been a basic design criterion.[10]

General S. E. Anderson, Commander of the Air Materiel Command, strongly seconded this position on 1 May 1959, when he called upon the Air Force Chief of Staff for a firm commitment concerning the use of high energy fuels over the next seven years. General Anderson pointed out that a five tons-per-day production facility would be operative by July 1959, but this plant could not supply the needs of operational B-70 bombers. Furthermore, the fuel produced would be the interim HEF-3. HEF-4, suitable for use in both afterburner and main engine, was being produced only in pilot-plant quantities. General Anderson anticipated that production costs could eventually drop to $1 per pound for full-scale production. He called for an immediate decision on firm high energy fuel requirements to provide "maximum flexibility and overall economy."[11]

---

* This led to HEF becoming known as "zip fuels" in most later literature; however, the term was seldom used at the time and almost never in official writings.
† Boron oxide was a viscous liquid, melting at about 900 degF, and fluid to temperatures over 3,000 degF.

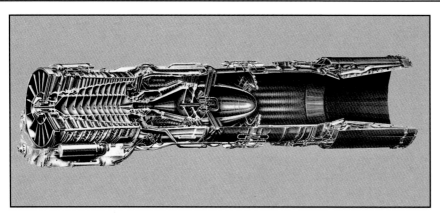

The J93-GE-5 did not look any different from the –3 engine but was equipped to burn HEF-3 in the afterburner. (General Electric Aircraft Engines)

In contrast to Secretary Horner's recommendation, the B-70 Project Office on 24 February 1959 urged the Strategic Air Command to make a "realistic evaluation" of the B-70's operational advantages with high energy fuel, since the Air Force program would soon come to the point where further direction was necessary. The Project Office reminded SAC that budgeting for high energy fuel production facilities had to be accomplished no later than FY60 so that engineering and construction could begin by January 1961. Only in this fashion could special-fuel production meet the needs of the first inventory vehicles. The Project Office underscored the interrelationship of timely fuel production and a successful high energy fuel engine program, noting that the latter was, in February 1958, ahead of schedule.[12]

A continuing lag in high-level decisions on the fuel program led the Air Materiel Command at the end of April 1959 to notify North American of a six month slippage in the J93-GE-5 engine program. By this time North American had already converted the second weapons bay into extra fuel tankage to enable the early B-70s to meet their range requirement using the new JP-6 fuel then being produced.[13]

After studying feasibility and cost data, in late May SAC recommended that first allocations of high energy fuel should aim at qualification of the J93-GE-5 engine, that the first B-70 operational wing should have the –5 (rather than the –3) engine to prevent costly future modifications, and that high energy fuel – though its cost was competitive – should not exclude other means of range extension. Noting that the B-70 should exceed minimum range requirements even with the new JP-6, SAC emphasized that the new fuel would allow greater target coverage, heavier payloads, better penetration routes, a choice of recovery bases, and more adequate landing reserves.[14]

These advantages would accrue despite 1,620 pounds added to the total weight of the aircraft. When both engine sections used JP-6, this weight penalty would result in only a 75 mile range degradation. Moreover, properly metered high energy fuel flow rates would provide the same exhaust gas temperature as with JP-6. In the dual-fuel configuration, high energy fuels would require between 30 and 40 percent of the total fuel capacity. Finally, the two type of fuel would have separate sequenc-

ing, pressurization, and venting systems which could be integrated – as desired –for all-JP-6 missions.[15]

During 1958 "immeasurable gains" marked the solution of practical and technical problems related to the production of high energy fuels. The feasibility of producing high energy fuels consistently and on a large scale was also definitely established.[16]

On 8 July 1959 the ARDC, AMC, and SAC made a joint presentation on high energy fuels to the Air Force Weapons Board. The board chairman, Colonel J. C. Jennison, recommended a continued authorization of J93-GE-5 engine development, inclusion in the FY61 budget of funds for the first 10-tons-per-day fuel facility, an allocation of $3.75 million for an all-HEF engine development feasibility study in FY60, and the provision of $27.6 million in FY60 for fuel purchases to support the current engine developmental program. There were no recommendations, however, to commit the B-70 to high energy fuels.[17]

On 16 July 1959 Air Force Headquarters authorized purchases of the new fuels in FY60, but on 10 August the Pentagon unexpectedly drastically reduced the over-all scope of the high energy fuel endeavor and cancelled the J93-GE-5 engine program. The motives were somewhat unclear, but included a general lack of interest, fiscal constraints, and environmental concerns.[18]

Cancellation of the –5 engine definitely limited B-70 planning to an engine using only JP-type fuels, and this restriction in turn forced North American to embark upon a redesign of the B-70's fuel system. People that actually witnessed the tests of the boron-burning J93-GE-5 seem to remember the exhaust the most. Apparently the high energy fuel burned very black, pouring a steady stream of smoke from the afterburner. The fuel also resulted in potentially worrisome borate deposits on the walls of the afterburner and exhaust nozzle.[19]

[1] Memorandum, E. A. Wolfe, Chief of Plans, Power Plant Laboratory, to Director of Weapon System Operations, WADC, Subject: Review of Strategic Bomber Capabilities, 27 June 1955; Memorandum, Chief of the Power Plant Laboratory, to Director of Weapon System Operations, WADC, Subject: Work Statement for Design Competition for Chemically-Powered Strategic Bomber System 110A, 6 June 1955. [2] Directive, Lieutenant Colonel D. F. Good, Chief 110A WSPO, to Chief, Propulsion Laboratory, WADC, Subject: High Energy Fuel Development Program, 21 April 1955; Directive, M. P. Dunnam, Chief, Fuel and Oil Branch, Propulsion Laboratory, to Chief 110A WSPO, WADC, Subject: High Energy Fuel Development Program, 16 may 1955. In the files of the AFMC History Office. [3] Directive, D. M. Ross Chief Operations Office, Propulsion Laboratory, WADC, to Chief 110A WSPO, Subject: Use of HEF-3 in WS-110A, 30 November 1956; WADC Tech Note 57-123, March 1957. [4] Letter, Colonel E. R. Lawrence, Assistant Director for Research and Development, USAF, to Commander ARDC, Subject: Air Force Engine Program for High Energy Fuel, 1 July 1957. [5] Directive, T. H. Goss, Assistant Chief, 110A WSPO, to Chief, Operations Division, WADC, Subject: HEF Program, 28 January 1958. [6] Letter, G. C. Rapp, Manager, J93 Aircraft Programs, GE, to Commander ARDC, Subject: J93 All HEF Feasibility Program, 16 June 1958; Letter, Harrison A. Storms, Chief Engineer, North American Aviation, to Commander AMC, Subject: All HEF B-70, 1 April 1959; Memorandum Colonel E. L. Bishop, Chief, B-70 WSPO, to Chief, Turbojet and Ramjet Engine Branch, Propulsion Laboratory, WADC, Subject: All HEF Turbojet Engine Feasibility Investigation, 13 April 1959; TWX, RDZSSL-30725-E, Director of Systems Management, ARDC, to Chief of Staff USAF, 28 May 1958. [7] WADC Weekly Tech Info report, 7 July 1958. [8] B-70 HEF Program Summary, 28 November 1958. in the files of the AFMC History Office. [9] Memorandum, R. E. Horner, Assistant Secretary for Research and Development, to Chief of Staff USAF, 12 February 1959. In the files of the Air Force History office. [10] Letter, General T. S. Power, Commander-in-Chief, SAC, to Chief of Staff USAF, Subject: Diversion of High Energy Fuel Program, 25 March 1959. [11] Letter, General S. E. Anderson, Commander AMC, to Chief of Staff USAF, Subject: High energy Fuel Program, 1 may 1959. [12] Letter, T. H. Goss, Assistant Chief B-70 WSPO, ARDC, to Commander-in-Chief SAC, Subject: B-70 HEF Program, 24 February 1959. [13] TWX, LMSA-4-1183, Commander AMC, to North American Aviation, 30 April 1959. [14] Letter, General T. S. Power, Commander-in-Chief SAC, to Chief of Staff USAF, Subject: Application of High Energy Fuel to the B-70, 25 may 1959. [15] B-70 HEF Program Summary, 28 November 1958. [16] History report, Propulsion Laboratory, WADC, July-December 1958. [17] Systems Management Division (ARDC) Weekly Activity Report, 24 July 1959. [18] TWX, AFMTPEO-6-2294, Chief of Staff USAF, to Commander ARDC, 10 August 1959. [19] Aviation Week, 17 August 1959; Aviation Week, 31 august 1959; Aviation Week, 7 September 1959; New York Times, 12 August 1959.

NORTH AMERICAN SST

AN XB-70-DERIVED PROTOTYPE

On 7 July 1961 North American released the results of a study into possible development plans for an early American supersonic transport (SST). The internally-funded study had been conducted to aid the Federal Aviation Agency (FAA – it became an Administration later) in establishing the development plan for an eventual SST. The study assumed that the primary goal would be to develop a supersonic aircraft suitable for general airline passenger service and economically competitive with existing transport aircraft. Keep in mind that the first American jetliner, the Boeing 707, had only been in commercial service for two years, and the politically-troubled Boeing SST project was still several years in the future.[1]

The North American study concentrated on the best way to develop the infrastructure necessary to support an SST, not necessarily on a definitive design for a production aircraft. The company realized that the development of an SST involved a broad spectrum of technical, economic, and practical problems. Many of these problems could be solved by incorporating the proper qualities and characteristics into the aircraft, but others required operational solutions – such as research into sonic booms, air traffic control, airports and terminal facilities, and operating policies, procedures, and regulations.[2]

By 1961, North American felt that the national investment in a commercial SST had already progressed considerably. They cited, as examples, the research necessary to produce supersonic fighters, and the development of the Convair B-58 Hustler medium bomber, which was the first long-range supersonic aircraft developed in the United States. The B-58's fuel consumption at supersonic speeds was considerably better than previous aircraft, but the basic design was "essentially a compromise between efficient subsonic and supersonic performance." An aircraft designed for an all-supersonic mission could do better. This was the same conclusion reached during the early WS-110A split-mission studies.[3]

The concept of achieving efficient supersonic cruise by eliminating compromises for subsonic performance was first applied to the design of the XB-70A. Supersonic cruise efficiency was improved to the extent that the range of the aircraft at Mach

3 speeds was comparable to subsonic aircraft of similar gross weights. North American believed that the B-70 would provide a basis for a useful research aircraft, while admitting that it was a less than ideal configuration for any eventual production SST. They were quick to point out that the United States government had already invested over $500 million in technology to support the B-70 program; an amount that could be quickly leveraged to develop an SST technology demonstrator.[4]

Unusually for an aerospace company, North American wanted a cautious approach, recognizing that it would not result in an operational aircraft in the immediate future. "This position presupposes that the primary objective is a profitable commercial transport, and that a plan is desired which balances urgency, risk, and cost to the extent that undue risk and excessive development costs are avoided. If any national objectives, such as prestige or military desirability, should shift the balance so that urgency became the dominant consideration, with cost and risk being minor factors, then obviously it would be possible to develop an SST somewhat earlier than the plans presented in this report."[5]

The report went on to describe three possible approaches of achieving the primary objective of a safe, profitable, supersonic transport for commercial airline service. The approaches were called: (1) production prototype, (2) experimental prototype, and (3) military or civil cargo prototype. Also described were two B-70 operational test vehicle programs that could be implemented.[6]

North American proposed to build two additional XB-70 airframes, modified for use as SST development hacks. These aircraft could have flown, according to North American estimates, four years earlier than any possible purpose-designed SST prototype, allowing a great deal of time to evaluate areas of interest to the SST designers.[7]

SST ENGINE TESTBED

One of the modified XB-70s would be used to provide a flying testbed for new SST engines. Although the General Electric J93 turbojet used in the B-70 was one of the keys to its great performance, it was already acknowledged that the J93 (and its Pratt & Whitney J58 pseudo-backup program) would not be sufficient reliable or economical for commercial service. Because of this,

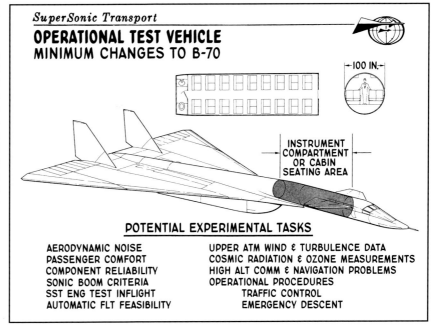

A chart showing the potential uses of an operational test vehicle based on the XB-70A. (North American Aviation)

the government had begun financing the advanced Lightweight Gas Generator Program and had awarded contracts to both General Electric and Pratt & Whitney. The supersonic gas generator being developed could be adapted to several different engine cycles – turbofan, fan with duct burning, turboramjet, etc.[8]

North American believed it was essential to gain flight experience with the new engine before the first prototype SST was completed – an excellent idea given the problems encountered with the JTD9 turbofan on the subsonic 747 a few years later. To accomplish this, they proposed modifying one of the additional XB-70 airframes to carry a single SST engine in place of two of the regular J93s. This would leave three J93s on one side and the outboard J93 on the other side, allowing the aircraft to fly under any conditions without the use of the SST engine. Modifications would needed to the internal ducting to accommodate the increased mass flow required by the new SST engine; minor modifications to the external mold line would also be necessary to accommodate the increased diameter expected of the new engine.[9]

Alternately, one of the SST engines could be mounted underneath the fuselage. This was essential if the final design required externally mounting the engines – much like the eventual Boeing SST design. In this case, flight testing the inlet configurations and nacelle shapes would be necessary. The engine would be mounted on a pylon that could be partially retracted into what had been designed as the weapons bay to minimize clearance problems during takeoff and landing. The engine would be equipped with a particular inlet design to evaluate engine performance at a particular design point speed. Alternate inlet designs could be tested, but not during a single flight.[10]

PROTOTYPE SST

The second XB-70 airframe would be modified to a limited passenger configuration by removing the military electronics and fuel from the upper fuselage ("neck") and replacing it with a small passenger compartment. The fuel would either be moved into the area previously occupied by the weapons bay in the lower fuselage, or just simply be deleted and the range penalty accepted for the demonstration vehicle.[11]

Without changing the mold line of the upper fuselage, a total of 36 passenger could be accommodated in 4-abreast seating. The internal diameter of the fuselage was only 100 inches – four feet narrower than the contemporary Boeing 707. A single restroom would be located at the extreme rear of the passenger compartment. Interestingly, a galley was not included, partially because of a lack of room, and partially because all flights were expected to be so short as to eliminate the need for one. Two versions of this design were proposed. The first simply eliminated the fuel normally carried in the upper fuselage. This version had a gross takeoff weight of 337,000 pounds and a range of 2,900 miles. The second version moved 47,400 pounds of fuel into the weapons bay (for a total of 185,000 pounds) and resulted in an aircraft weighing 384,500 pounds with a range of just over 4,000 miles. Passenger ingress and egress, as well as emergency evacuation, would be complicated by the height of the XB-70 fuselage.[12]

Two other configurations were also proposed that slightly changed the outer mold line, but provided more realistic passenger counts. Both included the weapons bay fuel. The first extended the internal passenger compartment by 240 inches, resulting in seating for 48 passengers. This version had a gross takeoff weight of 427,000 pounds and could fly 3,850 miles while cruising at Mach 3. The other version increased the passenger compartment another 264 inches (for a total stretch of 504 inches) to seat 76 passengers. The gross takeoff weight increased to 461,000 pounds, but range was reduced to only 3,600 miles at Mach 3. Neither modification changed the overall length of the fuselage, but rather resulted in a more pronounced "hump" in the rear part of the neck. The expected effect on stability was thought to be negligible, but given the marginal directional stability of the XB-70 in any case, the modifications would probably have necessitated an increase in vertical stabilizer area.[13]

North American's rationale for using an XB-70 as an early SST demonstrator had several valid points. The primary contribution was identified as the early definition of problems associated with the operation of an SST, made possible by limited passenger flights as early as 1965. Since the FAA would not have certificated the aircraft, they would probably have been limited to military or government (NASA, etc.) operations. The expected problems included air traffic control, airport operations, maintenance, scheduling, etc. Sufficient lead-time was available to resolve these problems in an efficient and orderly manner before large numbers of SSTs were produced. Regulations and systems could be developed to monitor and control the operations of supersonic aircraft by the time production aircraft were introduced into airline service. The FAA could use the early service experience to write new Federal Air Regulations covering the certification process and design criteria for supersonic transports.[14]

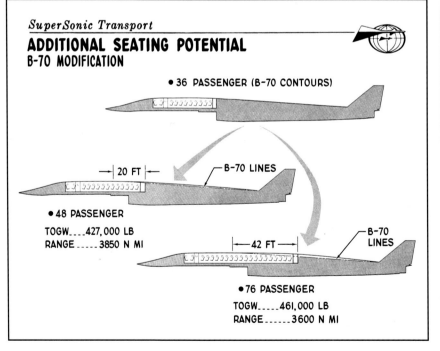

Several schemes were put forth to use the basic XB-70A airframe as an early prototype SST. (North American Aviation)

It would be possible to accumulate 4,000–5,000 flight hours of experience prior to the beginning of FAA certification tests on the final SST. The XB-70-derived SST could demonstrate the feasibility of basic concepts associate with intercontinental supersonic aircraft, general performance characteristics, flight characteristics, and subsystem component reliability of an aircraft of comparable size and speed capability. The aircraft could also provide in-flight testing and evaluation of SST engines, environmental systems, navigation equipment, and other subsystems. North American also pointed out that early flights of a supersonic transport might be in the national interest from the standpoint of international prestige since the United States could "claim" to have an operable SST at a very early date.[15]

POSSIBLE SST DESIGN

Engineers being engineers, the Preliminary Design Department could not resist putting forth their own conceptual design for an SST. Surprisingly, it bore little resemblance to the XB-70, except for the extreme forward fuselage that was obviously inspired by the Valkyrie's neck. The resulting aircraft was 198 feet long, 31 feet high, and had a 192-foot wingspan. The gross takeoff weight was estimated at 450,000 pounds, and between 100 and 150 passengers could be carried at Mach 2 cruising speeds for 4,000 miles. It was thought that a prototype of this aircraft could be completed within 6 years (1967) and that the design could be certificated by 1973.[16]

North American believed that 12 prototypes should be constructed and used primarily as military or civilian cargo transports to gain experience with the design before committing it to production. This explains the very long (7,000 flight hour) certification period. This use was proposed because it was believed that both the FAA and the insurance companies would object to carrying civilian passengers on what amounted to experimental aircraft. The government, airlines, and insurance companies still remembered the unhappy experience with the first commercial jetliner – the de Havilland Comet. It was also acknowledged that any civilian cargo operations using the aircraft would most probably lose money since the operating costs were expected to be higher than subsonic air-freighters.[17]

North American also extrapolated the general characteristics of a commercial SST into a MATS (Military Air Transport Ser-

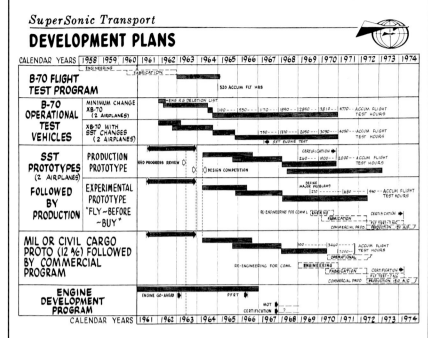

vice) supersonic logistics aircraft. North American believed that the fuselage cross-section preferred for a commercial transport was satisfactory to perform many MATS missions such as the transportation of troops or dependents, or carrying military limited-war cargo on standard 98x108-inch pallets. It was decided to optimize the design as a commercial passenger transport, and then develop the necessary modifications, primarily to permit cargo loading, to allow a reasonable MATS transport to emerge.[18]

North American investigated several options for providing cargo access to the aircraft, including a swinging nose door, a nose ramp, and a traditional side cargo door. The nose ramp emerged as the most practical; it provided more loading flexibility than the side cargo door and was less complex than the swinging nose door. Since this configuration was almost identical to the aerodynamic shape of the assumed commercial SST, the re-engineering necessary to change the aircraft from a MATS configuration to one suitable for commercial passenger operations was minimal. The experience gained from limited MATS service were therefore directly applicable to the final commercial version.[19]

During a limited (non-nuclear) war, the supersonic transport could support modern high-performance combat forces immedi-

ately, anywhere in the world. North American pointed out that the then-new supersonic retaliatory and strike forces were supported by low-speed subsonic transports, and believed that strategic and tactical forces should be supported, at least in critical areas, by transport aircraft of equal speed capabilities. The basic design required runways 5,500 feet long, and could transport 40,000 pounds of cargo 3,000 nm at over Mach 2.[20]

SUMMARY

In the end, no action was taken on North American's proposal, although some of the experiments they proposed for the two additional XB-70 aircraft (sonic boom measurements, subsystems development, etc.) were actually performed much later on the two Air Force-NASA XB-70As. The cost and political turmoil surrounding the B-70 program fairly much guaranteed that they could not be used directly as SST prototypes. Eventually, the FAA and NASA would undertake the development of a commercial SST with Lockheed and Boeing playing major roles, but again, cost and political turmoil would end the program before any significant hardware was built. The Soviet Union and Europe would go on to build small SST fleets that proved to be very uneconomical and controversial. Forty years later, the world is still waiting for an American SST to appear.

---

[1] North American Report NA-61-367, Supersonic Transport Development Plans Study, 7 July 1961. [2] Ibid. [3] Ibid. [4] Ibid. [5] Ibid. [6] Ibid. [7] Ibid. [8] Ibid. [9] Ibid. [10] Ibid. [11] Ibid. [12] Ibid. [13] Ibid. [14] Ibid. [15] Ibid. [16] Ibid. [17] Ibid. [18] Ibid. [19] Ibid. [20] Ibid.

SIGNIFICANT DATES

1947
The Air Force begins developing requirements for a supersonic bomber.

14 October 1947
Chuck Yeager makes first intentional supersonic flight in the Bell XS-1.

30 March 1953
The Strategic Air Command requests the development of a supersonic bomber

1 May 1953
Boeing is issued a contract to study a supersonic intercontinental bomber

October 1954
The Air Force issues GOR 38 for a high-speed intercontinental bomber

29 December 1954
The Air Council authorizes the development of a chemically-powered bomber as WS-110A and a nuclear-powered bomber as WS-125A.

February 1955
GOR 96 is issued for a high-speed reconnaissance aircraft similar to GOR 38. The system is designated WS-110L.

18 February 1955
The Air Force issues SR 22 for a chemically-powered bomber possessing "maximum possible speed."

22 March 1955
GOR 82 supercedes GOR 38 calling for a bomber with the maximum possible "supersonic" speed over the target.

16 July 1955
Six airframe contractors – Boeing, Convair, Douglas, Lockheed, Martin, and North American – are asked to bid on the WS-110A/L aircraft. Only Boeing and North American express an interest.

6 October 1955
GOR 114 is issued for the WS-202A Mach 3 interceptor that will become the XF-108.

8 November 1955
Boeing and North American are awarded WS-110A/L development contracts.

September 1956
The Boeing and North American designs are rejected and the contractors advised to "return to the drawing boards."

6 June 1957
North American Aviation receives a contract to develop the XF-108 all-weather two-man Mach 3 interceptor.

26 July 1957
General Electric is awarded a contract to develop the J93 engine that will power the WS-110A aircraft.

18 October 1957
Boeing and North American submit revised proposal for the WS-110A/L.

23 December 1957
North American is announced as the winner of the WS-110A/L competition.

February 1958
The WS-110A aircraft is designated B-70. Later the same month, the WS-110L reconnaissance aircraft is cancelled.

3 July 1958
The B-70 is named Valkyrie.

26 January 1959
The XF-108 mockup is inspected at the North American plant in Inglewood.

30 March 1959
The B-70 mockup is reviewed at the North American plant in Inglewood.

15 May 1959
The XF-108 is named Rapier.

10 August 1959
The high energy fuel program is cancelled, and long with it the J93-GE-5 engine for the B-70.

23 September 1959
The XF-108 project is cancelled.

1 December 1959
The B-70 program is reduced to a single prototype and most subsystem development is cancelled entirely.

August 1960
The B-70 program is restructured into a weapons system development effort and 11 YB-70 service test aircraft are ordered in addition to the one XB-70 prototype.

31 March 1961
The program is reduced again, this time to three prototypes plus the IBM bombing and navigation system.

11 May 1964
A/V-1 is rolled out in Palmdale.

21 September 1964
The maiden flight of A/V-1. All did not go according to plan.

12 October 1964
A/V-1 breaks the sound barrier for the first time, on her third flight.

25 October 1964
A/V-1 returns to Palmdale for structural testing.

16 February 1965
Testing complete, A/V-1 makes her fifth test flight.

29 May 1965
A/V-2 is rolled out in Palmdale.

17 July 1965
A/V-1 makes her first flight, breaking the sound barrier at 42,000 feet.

14 October 1965
A/V-1 records Mach 3.02 at 70,000 feet – the first Mach 3 flight of the program, and the last for A/V-1 due to concerns her honeycomb skin will separate at high speeds.

3 January 1966
A/V-2 reaches Mach 3.05.

24 March 1966
The airshow at Carswell AFB, Texas, is visited by A/V-2 – the only time a B-70 landed someplace besides Edwards or Palmdale (except for the last flight).

19 May 1966
A/V-2 flies at Mach 3.006 for 33 minutes.

6 June 1966
The National Sonic Boom Program begins.

8 June 1966
A mid air collision kills A/V-2 copilot Carl Cross and F-104 pilot Joe Walker, and results in the loss of the second XB-70A.

13 January 1969
NASA announces the XB-70A program is being terminated.

4 February 1969
The last flight of A/V-1 – to the Air Force Museum at Wright-Patterson AFB, Ohio.